*We dedicate this book
to anyone who has the courage
to change their thinking
so that together,
we can improve ourselves
and change the world.*

THINK GEN WHY

KYLER GRAFF • JESSE WRIGHT
MATTHEW WOOD • RYAN MILLER
ETHAN JONES • J. ERIC WRIGHT

Copyright © 2018
by Think Gen Why, LLC

ISBN-13: 978-0-9967836-2-0
ISBN-10: 0-9967836-2-8

Version 2018.01.1 | January 2018

All rights reserved. No part of this publication may be reproduced, distributed, or transmitted in any form or by any means, including photocopying, recording, or other electronic or mechanical methods, without the prior written permission of the publisher, except in the case of brief quotations embodied in critical reviews and certain other non-commercial uses permitted by copyright law. For permission requests, write to the publisher at the address below, or email: TGY@davidstrauss.com

Think Gen Why, LLC
c/o David Strauss
PO Box 28
Boulder, Colorado 80306

Ordering Information:
Special discounts are available on quantity purchases by corporations, associations, and organizations.
Retail orders on Amazon.com or ThinkGenWhyBook.com

Contact the publisher at the above address for special discounts.

Cover Photo: Jonathan Castner Photography
Cover Design: Spare Design | Barbara Wade
Copy Editor: | Aaron Sullivan

A Giggle Yoga Project Production
www.GiggleYoga.com

"If parents want to give their children a gift, the best thing they can do is to teach their children to love challenges, be intrigued by mistakes, enjoy effort, and keep on learning. That way, their children don't have to be slaves of praise. They will have a lifelong way to build and repair their own confidence."
— Carol S. Dweck

TABLE OF CONTENTS

INTRODUCTION TO THINK GEN WHY   11

BOOK ONE
FROM DIRT ROAD TO HIGHWAY
BY: KYLER GRAFF

FROM DIRT ROAD TO HIGHWAY	15
PROLOGUE	17
LESSON ONE: It Is Good to Be Different	21
LESSON TWO: Surround Yourself With the Right People	25
LESSON THREE: You Have to Make Things Happen	29
LESSON FOUR: Get Outside of Your Comfort Zone	33
LESSON FIVE: Pivot in a New Direction	37
LESSON SIX: Be Grateful	41
EPILOGUE	43
ACKNOWLEDGEMENTS	47

BOOK TWO
PERFECTLY IMPERFECT
BY: JESSE WRIGHT

PERFECTLY IMPERFECT	49
PROLOGUE	51
LESSON ONE: Have the Courage to Be Yourself	55
LESSON TWO: Change Your Mindset, Change Your Life	59
LESSON THREE: Be the Leader of Your Own Life	67
LESSON FOUR: Develop a Winning Mindset	73
EPILOGUE	81
ACKNOWLEDGEMENTS	83

TABLE OF CONTENTS

BOOK THREE
YOU ARE THE WALL
BY: MATTHEW WOOD

YOU ARE THE WALL	85
PROLOGUE	87
LESSON ONE: Change Your Story, Change Your Life	89
LESSON TWO: Forgiveness Is the Ultimate Solvent	95
LESSON THREE: Identify Your "Why"	97
LESSON FOUR: Turn Your Bricks Into Bridges	101
LESSON FIVE: Be Grateful	105
EPILOGUE	107
ACKNOWLEDGEMENTS	109

BOOK FOUR
SLACKLINER'S MINDSET
BY: RYAN MILLER

SLACKLINER'S MINDSET	111
PROLOGUE	113
INTRO TO THE SLACKLINER'S MINDSET	115
LESSON ONE: Stay Focused	119
LESSON TWO: Be Persistent	127
LESSON THREE: Build Your Confidence	133
LESSON FOUR: Find Your Balance	141
LESSON FIVE: Maintain a Positive Outlook .	147
LESSON SIX: Live in the Moment	151
LESSON SEVEN: Learn From Successful People	157
EPILOGUE	163
ACKNOWLEDGEMENTS	167

TABLE OF CONTENTS

BOOK FIVE
THE FAITH CODE
BY: ETHAN JONES

THE FAITH CODE	169
PROLOGUE	171
LESSON ONE: Be Open to Making Changes	175
LESSON TWO: Commit to Personal Growth	181
LESSON THREE: Be Coachable	189
LESSON FOUR: Develop a Healthy Mindset	195
LESSON FIVE: Take Responsibility for Your Outcome	203
EPILOGUE	209
ACKNOWLEDGEMENTS	213

BOOK SIX
DOUBLE DOWN
BY: J. ERIC WRIGHT

DOUBLE DOWN	215
PROLOGUE	217
LESSON ONE: Cultivate a Family Environment	223
LESSON TWO: Double Down on What You Are Good At	231
LESSON THREE: When the Going Gets Tough, Get Focused	237
LESSON FOUR: Turn Challenges Into Opportunities	243
EPILOGUE	249
ACKNOWLEDGEMENTS	253

CREDITS

AFTERWORD	257
JOIN THE THINK GEN WHY MOVEMENT	259
A CALL TO ACTION	261
ABOUT THE COACH	263
THANK YOU TO OUR SPONSORS	265

Introduction

Have you ever wondered how different our world would be if our educational systems went beyond teaching the basics and actually taught success skills for life?

The six authors of *Think Gen Why* asked themselves this question at a young age, and they discovered a whole new way of thinking that was not taught in schools. They came together in their teens and 20s to write this book because they are enthusiastic about sharing what they have learned and want to make a difference in the world.

These young men discovered that the solution to any challenge could be found by looking in the mirror and exploring your thoughts and beliefs. They also realized that the shortest path to success is to develop a greater sense of self-awareness and personal responsibility and to learn how to think and make decisions by following the advice of people who have already succeeded.

Through their personal stories, each of these young men wants to motivate and inspire their generation and anyone else with an open mind, to get off the excuse train and start taking responsibility for the direction of their life. They want their readers to realize that if you want to change the direction of your life, you can. You do not have to be the same person tomorrow that you are today. All it takes is having the courage to let go of old ideas and try something new.

Here are some of the thoughts that they write about:

KYLER GRAFF
- It is good to be different
- Surround yourself with the right people
- You have to make things happen
- Get outside of your comfort zone
- Pivot in a new direction
- Be grateful

Jesse Wright
- Have the courage to be yourself
- Change your mindset, change your life
- Raise your people standards
- Be the leader of your own life
- Develop a winning philosophy

Matthew Wood
- Change your story, change your life
- Forgiveness is the ultimate solvent
- Identify your why
- Turn your bricks into bridges
- Live with gratitude

Ryan Miller
- Have an end goal in mind
- Create a plan and take action
- Overcome the wobbles
- Ditch your excuses
- Keep your eyes on your goal
- Stay calm

Ethan Jones
- Be open to making changes
- Commit to personal growth
- Be a coachable person
- Develop a healthy mindset
- Take responsibility for your outcome

J. Eric Wright
- Cultivate a family environment
- Double down on what you are good at
- When the going gets tough, get focused
- Turn challenges into opportunities

No matter what your age or life conditions, no matter what your childhood was like, if you are willing to improve your thinking and shift your perspective, a new road of possibilities awaits you, and it starts with reading this book and applying the lessons that are shared.

*"You will never follow
your own inner voice
until you clear up
the doubts in your mind."
— Roy T. Bennett*

BOOK ONE

FROM DIRT ROAD TO HIGHWAY

SIX LESSONS TO PAVE THE ROAD TO YOUR FUTURE

• KYLER GRAFF •

Prologue

"It had long since come to my attention that people of accomplishment rarely sat back and let things happen to them.
They went out and happened to things."
— Leonardo da Vinci

Have you ever been curious about what separates those people who always seem to get everything they want from the ones who believe that life is hard and the world is against them?

When I first asked myself this question, it was because while I was growing up, I was very unhappy and did not care about anything. I appeared happy on the outside but was actually struggling with my self-image on the inside. You can probably guess what my mental programming was: I thought the world was against me. I thought my parents were against me, and I thought my teachers were against me. I hated my life. I was always complaining and continuously asked myself "why me?" It was a tough mindset to live with every day, and I knew I did not want to live that way forever. Something had to change.

Looking back at the early years of my life, my parents gave me a great childhood. They did the best with what they had, but they did not understand what was going on in my head or how to control me. I was always getting into trouble for something stupid. In high school, I was suspended for streaking at the Homecoming football game. My parents did not know what to do with me. I remember when they became so frustrated that they told me they were thinking about sending me to military school. Thankfully, that never happened. But then, during my junior year, I got in trouble again, and my parents took everything away from me—my car, my phone, my friends. It sucked!

When I look back on all my troubles, the questions that come to mind are why did I not care about anything, and why did I have such a bad self-image?

Growing up, I saw myself as being different from everyone else and thought it was a bad thing. I never felt like I fit in anywhere, not even with my friends or family. School was never my thing. I was easily distracted and found it very difficult to keep up with the pace of classes, and so my grades were not that good. I was always comparing myself to people who I saw as being better than me. I was envious of them because I wanted to be like them, but I never believed I could be. Only in a dream world was that possible.

Things got so bad in my mind that I almost did not graduate high school. It was our English class senior project that we were supposed to have been working on all semester that almost caused me to flunk. I had not even started working on my senior project when the day came to turn it in, so I called in sick to school. I did not care about anything. I just wanted to be out of the "prison" school system. We were supposed to graduate in two days, and I was failing my English class. Thank God I did a lot of selling growing up because I was able to convince my teacher to let me present the project to him directly instead of to the class. I needed to have 60% or higher grade to pass. I ended up barely passing with a 60.01%. My teacher either liked me or felt sorry for me. Regardless, I was able to wear the cap and gown and walk across the stage at Red Rocks Amphitheatre.

At my graduation party, everyone was asking me where I was going to go to college. I remember saying Arapahoe Community College. Deep inside, it did not feel right. I ended up signing up to attend and even went to orientation. While sitting in orientation and listening to the cranky monotone voice talk about the basics of being a freshman, I thought to myself, "Wow, am I really about to go to college here?" I left that day and never returned. I still believed very strongly in being educated, but I had to create my own path and find my own way.

Since I decided not to go to college, I used the money I received at graduation for a different purpose. Instead of spending my graduation gift money on school supplies, I used the money to get involved in a network marketing company that offered a lot of personal development training. It was there that I was introduced to a new way of thinking that has set me on the path of being a young entrepreneur and led me to become a co-author of this book.

I have consolidated my new way of thinking into six core lessons which have revolutionized who I am today:

1) It is good to be different
2) Surround yourself with the right people
3) You have to make things happen
4) Get outside of your comfort zone
5) Pivot in a new direction
6) Be grateful

As I share my insights on these six lessons, I challenge you to reflect upon your own life and how they may apply to you.

LESSON ONE

IT IS GOOD TO BE DIFFERENT

"The person who follows the crowd will usually go no further than the crowd. The person who walks alone is likely to find himself in places no one has ever seen before."
— Albert Einstein

What would your life be like if you did not have the constant pressure of wanting to be approved and accepted by others? What if you did not care what people thought about you? What if you realized that what matters most is what you think about yourself?

Until I was 18, I was always concerned about what other people thought about me, especially my friends. I felt like I always needed the approval from others just to fit in. If I did not have their approval, I would be down on myself and feel left out. I would have a "why me?" attitude that would make me feel isolated, insecure, and envious of others. No one ever taught me how to love and accept myself, and I was always looking for other people to validate and accept me.

After graduating from high school, even though college was off my radar and I had chosen to find a different path and work on my new mindset, I still felt like an outcast. All my friends were going to college, and I still yearned for their acceptance. I finally got out of that mental funk, and things started changing for me when I distanced myself from my friends, became more independent, and started working for a pipeline company in North Dakota.

While working in North Dakota, isolated from my familiar environment, I found myself in the perfect situation to get to know myself. I was making good money, and for the first time in my life, I could support myself financially, which gave me the time to think about who I am, what I want, and what I want my life to become. I was able to step back from all my distractions and take a close look at my life from the inside-out and be brutally honest with myself about my thoughts and feelings, strengths and weaknesses.

While reflecting on my past, I remembered that when I was working in the network marketing company one year prior, I had learned that all the successful leaders who had what I wanted were avid readers and always listened to personal development audio books while in their cars. They taught me that you could get the equivalent of a bachelor's degree in a single year by turning your driving time into a classroom. That is exactly what I did while working with the pipeline company.

I remember sitting in my white Chevy 2500 pickup driving around from job site to job site in frigid cold weather—but I did not care because it was my mobile classroom. Instead of listening to music on the radio, I flooded my mind with audio books that taught me how to build my self-confidence, become a better salesperson, and understand the psychology of how people think. This was my non-traditional way of learning how to become a successful entrepreneur. I was finally starting to feel good about my decision to run against the herd and not attend college, and I began feeling proud of myself for being a trailblazer in my own life. The more I listened and learned, the more I realized I was better off being unique and different in a world where everyone is trying to fit in.

With all this thinking and learning in my mobile classroom, I realized that I did not need the acceptance of others to create my own life. Instead, I wanted to become the person who helped others to love and accept themselves. With this thought, all my apprehension about not going to college melted away, and I began to feel like I owned my life and that I was no longer a prisoner of my past. I finally realized that it is a good thing to be different.

With this newfound confidence, I identified five questions that helped me embrace what is different about me and why I can succeed in anything I do.

1. What are my unique qualities?
2. What are my strengths and weaknesses?
3. What do I need to do to build my confidence?
4. How can I believe in myself?
5. How can I build my mental strength?

Each of these questions helped me empower myself, because when you ask the right questions, you set yourself up to win; your mind will always look for the answer to any question you ask of it. I used to ask myself negative questions that made me feel lousy about myself. "What's wrong with me? Why don't I have any friends? Why am I such a loser?"

With my new mindset, asking myself these better questions took me onto the next stage of my journey. I began aligning myself with people who could help me grow into the successful, influential man I see myself becoming.

LESSON TWO

SURROUND YOURSELF WITH THE RIGHT PEOPLE

*"If you hang out in a barber shop long enough,
you are bound to get a haircut."*
— *Unknown*

One of the most important lessons I learned while sitting in my Chevy 2500 classroom became the number one KEY to transforming my life from poor self-image to becoming a leader:

*The people and environment you surround yourself with
directly influence who you eventually become.*

Looking back on my school days, I switched around between a lot of different groups when I was looking for friends and acceptance. I went from the skater group, to the rollerblade group, to the video game group, to the Parkour group; from the hockey group, to the lacrosse group, to the party group, to the business group, to a filmmaking group. Each time I started to hang out with a different group, I would begin to do what the people in that group did so I would fit in with them. For instance, when I started hanging out with kids that skateboarded, I naturally wanted to skateboard. When I started hanging out with people doing Parkour, I started learning how to do flips, how to jump off parking garage buildings (without dying), and other crazy stunts. I must have liked Parkour the most—or it was the easiest way to get noticed—because I did some wacky stuff. The craziest thing I did was jump off a building that was almost two stories tall. After that, I scaled up the side of a three-story bridge with small grips. If I had fallen, it would have been to the rocks below and the end of my life.

Looking back on all the different groups I joined, it is clear to me now that the people and environment you surround yourself with directly influence who you eventually become. Even though I did not know it at the time, this is a fundamental principle of success. Find people who have what you want, then do what they do, and you will get their results.

If you hang with crazy people, you are bound to become crazy. If you hang out with people who have a go-getter and winner's attitude, you will take risks and think like a winner. The people you hang around with will rub off on you—the activities they do, their habits, their types of relationships, their mindset, how they treat other people, whether they are negative or optimistic. It is critically important to become aware of this because it will dictate where you are in five, 10, 15, and even 50 years down the road.

Another lesson I learned is that everything exists in terms of its opposite. For every yin, there is a yang, and for every yang, there is a yin. If there are people who can pull you down, there are also people who can lift you up. The people who lift you up are your mentors, role models, coaches, and the positive, inspiring people in your life. If you want to live a life where you are always moving up and forward you need to surround yourself with the right people. Ideally, you want to get a mentor and a coach.

A mentor is someone who has the results you want, and they are willing to teach you how to get those results. Since they have already been down the road you want to venture upon, they know what obstacles you will run into and can help you to navigate the challenges and blind spots. A coach is someone who can help you create strategies and action plans. They can challenge you mentally to help keep your thinking and mindset focused on the results you want to produce.

Finding the right mentor or coach is different for everyone. You have to find the people who match the direction you want to take your life.

I wanted to run my own business and be an inspiring entrepreneur to others. If I kept hanging out with the party crowd, would that have helped me achieve my goals? Of course not.

What I had to do was take inventory of who I was associating with on a daily basis and decide if they belonged in my life. I am not saying I had to cut everyone out of my life who was not exactly like me, but I did have to limit the amount of time I spent with the people who were not going where

I wanted to go. In their place, I sought out and found more like-minded people. I needed to bring more entrepreneurs into my life who wanted to change the world, so that is exactly what I did!

> *"I think it's important to get your surroundings as well as yourself into a positive state—meaning surround yourself with positive people, not the kind who are negative and jealous of everything you do."*
> — *Heidi Klum*

My first experience with surrounding myself with like-minded people was when I got involved with the networking company that was jam-packed with entrepreneurial-minded people who had a huge passion and vision for improving their lives. All those positive-minded, uplifting people rubbed off on me. I started thinking the way they were thinking and started changing the activities I was doing by listening to personal development books and attending conferences to better my life. I started thinking of ways to make money without working for someone else, and I began to identify mentors to bring into my life. The best part is that the people I chose to bring close to me became my support group. They understood what I wanted to do and why I did certain things, so naturally, they supported me on my journey.

When I started hanging out with the right people, it was as if my entire life took a quantum leap forward, all because I started to change my thinking. My old thinking was that of a scarcity mindset. I remember one time when I was with a friend from high school, and we went to a car dealership to look at a new car for him. He was looking at Lexus, BMW, and Mercedes. I remember asking him why he would spend all this money on one of these expensive cars when he could go buy a Honda for half the price, and it would be totally reliable. His mindset was different from mine. He had a higher standard for what was acceptable in his life, and he believed he could have it, which was very different from my mindset.

Since I believed it was not possible for me to have a nice car like that, I was unknowingly trying to suggest to him that he should get a cheaper car. What I was doing was being a naysayer and projecting my limiting beliefs onto him to influence his actions. I was thinking and acting like a crab in a bucket of water. When a crab is in a bucket of water, it cannot escape because the other crabs grab it and pull it back down to prevent the escape. This crab mentality is everywhere and can be easily recognized by some very common limiting beliefs.

"If I can't have it, neither can you."

"What if you fail?"

"Do not jump out of the bucket and take any risks because you might get hurt."

"Getting out of the bucket" can be an analogy for wanting to get a better job, move up the ladder in your career, improve your health or fitness, buy a bigger home, travel more, or any other improvement to your life. Whatever the bucket is, if you do not surround yourself with the right people who will encourage and inspire you, then you will find yourself with a bunch of crabs trying to drag you down and pull you back to their "reality."

In the book *Dancing with Vampires*, author David Strauss (who is also one of my coaches), refers to these crabs as *Energy Vampires*. He challenges you to stay away from the people and situations that suck the energy and enthusiasm out of you. If you do not, you stand the risk of having your happiness stolen from you. If you do stay away, you will see your life change for the better.

I know with absolute certainty that my reality started changing for the better when I stopped hanging out with crabs and started to change my thinking. I realized you have to be better than the crabs—smarter, more cooperative, more cunning, and more encouraging. If you want to climb out of your bucket, whatever it may be, do not let the other crabs pull you down. And if you are happy in your bucket but see someone else making a break for it, go ahead and give them a boost!

LESSON THREE

YOU HAVE TO MAKE THINGS HAPPEN

"If you cannot believe in miracles, then believe in yourself. When you want something bad enough, let that drive push you to make it happen. Sometimes you'll run into brick walls that are put there to test you. Find a way around them and stay focused on your dream. Where there's a will, there's a way."
— Isabel Lopez

Have you ever wondered why our school system only teaches us academics but never focuses on teaching us how to think strategically so that we can live up to our potential?

If I had known in high school what I know now about accurate, results-based thinking I would never have gone through all the emotional drama that plagued my childhood. One of the most valuable lessons I have learned since taking on the responsibility of advancing my education is that you cannot wait for your dreams to show up at your doorstep because they rarely will. Instead, you have to make things happen. Here are two steps I have learned to make things happen. They are a launchpad to your success.

1) Set goals and take action.
2) Get accountability partners.

SET GOALS AND TAKE ACTION

There are a lot of people preaching the belief that *you can have, do, or be anything you want,* but rarely do they give you a formula for making things happen. If you dig a bit deeper into that belief, what is actually being implied is that human potential is unlimited, but it is up to you to tap into that potential. If you do not tap into your potential, you take the risk of living a mediocre life or reaching the end of your life with regrets. If you do tap into your potential, you open yourself up to the possibility of having an extraordinary life. The choice you make comes down to your beliefs.

The challenge to self-actualizing what you are truly capable of is in believing that it is possible to reach a higher level of success. I work on my beliefs every day. I am both my best and worst critic. I believe that my potential is something that will always be there, right in front of me, inside of me. It's just a matter of gathering the willpower to overcome those negative thoughts—those pesky crabs—that tug away at my belief in what I can become.

Anyone who overcomes obstacles in their life first has to believe that they can do it, and then they have to move forward with conviction and push past their obstacles. They have to create a vision for what they want to do and where they want to go and break that vision down into S.M.A.R.T. goals.

- **S**pecific — Be clear about what you want
- **M**easurable — Identify progress points
- **A**ction Oriented — Establish specific actions steps
- **R**ealistic — Goals you want and believe in
- **T**ime bound — Set deadlines

I was first taught the S.M.A.R.T. goals formula by my grandpa, and it revolutionized my belief in how I could achieve what I set out to do and helped me track my progress along the way.

When I had gotten into trouble in high school and had everything taken away from me by my parents, my grandpa stepped in and started mentoring me. I was at rock bottom, and the only direction I had to go was up. I used this goal-setting strategy to bring me from ground zero to ground hero.

My parents were not sure how to handle me, so they had me do weekly meetings with my grandpa where he helped me set my first S.M.A.R.T. goals. My goals at the time were very small, but it was a huge stepping stone for me. I set goals to get a car, pay for a DECA.org leadership trip, to become an all-state lacrosse player, and even have better relationships with the people around me—all of which I achieved.

When my grandpa first asked me what five things I wanted to accomplish, it seemed like a foreign question to me. The thought of setting a goal and making it happen seemed crazy. I knew what I wanted, but I was not sure how to get it, and so I would get caught in the same loop that stops most people from setting goals. I would stop believing it was possible because I did not know how to make it a reality.

Here are the exact steps that my Grandpa took me through when he introduced me to S.M.A.R.T. goals:
1) Write a list of the things I want to achieve
2) Identify what tasks I would need to do to make it happen
3) Break down each task into weekly steps
4) Measure my progress
5) Set deadlines for accomplishment

After going through these first five steps, my Grandpa asked me the most important question:

Why do I want to achieve these goals?

After some thought, I told him that I wanted a car so I could be independent, and I wanted better relationships with my parents so I was not always fighting with them and getting yelled at.

With that, my Grandpa bestowed upon me the wisdom of how to get results. He said that it was important to know why you want something because that is what will give you the motivation to keep pressing forward on the days when you do not feel like putting in the work or effort. When you remember why you are doing something, if that reason is a strong enough action motivator, it will re-spark your engines and give you the drive to persist.

The *glue* to making all this work for me was the act of writing my goals on paper and making measurable action steps. Together, these increased my belief that my goals were possible and motivated me to take ACTION, which is the backbone of getting results.

When you are clear about what you want and why you want it, and you create action steps to follow, the path becomes so much clearer and easier to manage. You get excited, and you start working on getting things done. Where most people fall off track is when the excitement passes, and they lose track of their *why*.

GET ACCOUNTABILITY PARTNERS

The key to achieving S.M.A.R.T. goals is staying consistent and getting an accountability partner. This is someone who holds you to your commitments and does not listen to or accept your excuses for being inconsistent. You can be accountable to yourself, but when you have to be accountable to someone else, it takes your commitment to a whole new level.

My first accountability partner was my grandpa. Every week we would track my progress together. We would go through each goal and action step and check off whether I did it or not. As each week passed, I moved closer to my goals. Then I achieved my first one: I got a car. I was thinking—wow, this stuff works. Then shortly after that, I saved enough money to pay for my entire DECA trip. Then when I was a senior, I hit my goal of being an all-state lacrosse player.

To this day I continue to set S.M.A.R.T. goals in all areas of my life. In fact, that is how I started my first company, Pro Painters, an interior and exterior home painting company. When I was 20 years old, I set the goal of making Pro Painters a six-figure business. Within one year I hit that goal. Now I have set a bigger goal of turning it into a seven-figure business, and I am on track to reach or exceed that goal.

When I tell people they can have whatever they want in life, it is based on my own beliefs and experiences, and my results. I believe very strongly in S.M.A.R.T. goals and that you have to make things happen. When I first started making goals, I did not believe any of it was possible. But when I finally decided to take control of my life, I realized that anything is possible because my results reinforced my new beliefs.

LESSON FOUR

GET OUTSIDE OF YOUR COMFORT ZONE

"It's not the blowing of the wind that determines your destination, it's the set of the sail."
— Jim Rohn

What do you do when you know that you want to change the direction of your life, but you feel overwhelmed and stuck?

So many people go through life wanting things to change and improve, but not realizing that all change starts from within. In fact, most people want the world to change so that they do not have to. The reality is, you have to do something different to get a different result. It sounds simple, right? At face value, it is, but there is more to it.

If you want different results to show up in your life, you have to be willing to get outside your comfort zone, which can be very scary and intimidating because it takes you into the unknown. It is this fear of the unknown that stops a lot of people from taking action and keeps them mentally and emotionally stuck. People are afraid of all the negative "what ifs" that might happen instead of focusing on exactly what they want. They think, *"What if it doesn't work?"* instead of, *"What if it does work?"* Fears turn into excuses and excuses become a justification for not taking action.

I recently attended a conference titled "Destroying Excuses" which was presented by one of my mentors, Tony Grebmeier. At this event, I learned a simple and powerful technique to help anyone overcome the habit of making excuses. Tony taught us that we have to learn how to ask when we need help. For many people, asking for help is far outside their comfort zone, so they remain overwhelmed and stuck.

So many people, including myself, make assumptions and do not ask for help when we need it. We do not want to bother or inconvenience others so we sometimes tell ourselves, *"I do not really need help,"* or, *"I can do it on my own,"* or, *"They are too busy to help me."* Even more troubling, we may be afraid that people will judge us if they find out that we are having difficulties in our life, and we do not want to feel the shame or embarrassment of judgment. These assumptions are just bad mental programs. When we do not ask for help, we are not even giving people the chance to say yes or no.

After I had gone to this conference, I realized I was not asking for help because I did not want people to judge me when I felt weak or needed assistance. To get past that fear, I had to put my ego aside and start asking for help when I needed it.

Tony's simple lesson about *asking* has made it so much easier for me to improve my life. When I went to the "Destroying Excuses" conference, I had an inside advantage. I first met Tony several years earlier when I was working with the network marketing company, so I already knew he had credibility. He was one of the top leaders and had very impressive results. He had what I would consider to be the perfect family, nice cars, and everyone liked him. After meeting him in person, all I could think was that I wanted what he had. I was motivated by the fact that I had met someone who had the results I wanted, but shortly after that my negative programming kicked in and I thought there was no way I could be successful like him.

It was not just my negative thoughts; I had a lot of crabs in my life which pulled down and made me doubt myself. Thankfully, I got out of my comfort zone and stopped listening to the crabs and asked Tony if he could mentor me. He agreed, and that is when I first opened myself up to new possibilities.

For me, stepping into the unknown and meeting with Tony was a game changer. When we sat down for coffee, he told me I was very sharp and that he believed in me. Those two simple compliments made me believe in myself—something I had not done for a very long time. He told me to think big and that whatever I wanted I could have. All I had to do was go out and get it. He was right. That meeting with Tony left a
long-term impression upon me, giving me enthusiasm to be a self-reliant entrepreneur and pursue my dreams.

LESSON FOUR: GET OUTSIDE OF YOUR COMFORT ZONE

Looking back, up until the time when I first met Tony and was introduced to network marketing and the importance of reading and personal development, I had a warped view of successful people. I thought that the people who had money, nice cars, and picture-perfect families just got "lucky." Maybe there is some truth to that, but they created their luck. In the words of the granddaddy of personal development, Andrew Carnegie,

"Luck is when opportunity meets preparedness."
Or,
Luck = Opportunity + Preparedness

There are plenty of people who have been in the right place at the right time, but they weren't prepared, so they couldn't cash in on their luck.

I considered myself very lucky when I started working at the pipeline company in North Dakota. The opportunity was there, and I was fully prepared to commit to the career. It gave me financial stability and the opportunity to learn and grow in my mobile classroom. As much value as I gained from that experience, it was still a big company and did not allow me to indulge in my yearning to become an entrepreneur. Quite the opposite, I felt like a corporate slave. Based on everything I was learning at the time, I had to be true to myself and ditch my pipeline career to pursue my dreams. When I announced this to my family, they all turned into crabs. They wanted the best for me, and they truly thought that working for the pipeline was the best thing. This is where you have to believe in yourself. It was finally time for me to put to the test everything I had been learning about being an entrepreneur.

When I put in my two-week notice at work, a couple different bosses called me to say that I was making a huge mistake and that I was throwing away my future. From their point of view, I was, but in reality, I believed that my life was just now starting. They did not know I had a 100-year vision for my life, and that this job was just a stepping stone on the path to my success, and it was time for me to pivot in a new direction.

LESSON FIVE

PIVOT IN A NEW DIRECTION

*"We must have the courage to bet on our ideas,
to take the calculated risk, and to act.
Everyday living requires courage
if life is to be effective and bring happiness."*
— Maxwell Maltz

When you have a long-term vision for your life, the changes and adjustments that you make along the path of your success are not always big leaps or jumps. Sometimes they are pivots. A pivot is a calculated change in course. It is when you have one foot rooted in what you've learned thus far, and you fine-tune or change your strategy to reach the next level of success.

Every pivot I have taken in my life has been scary. I try and talk myself out of it every time. But there is this voice that always tells me to do it. I always ask myself if I would be okay lying on my death bed wondering what would have happened if I did not take that action step that forced me to make that calculated change. My rationale is that if life is a game and you win by trying new things, why not do it? Worst case scenario: I can go back to what I was doing.

My scariest pivot which changed everything in my life and has helped me become who I am today was when I decided to work for myself and quit my job at the pipeline company. When I lived in North Dakota, I was very content. I would wake up each day, work 10 to 12 hours, go home, go to the gym, eat, and then do the same thing the next day. Despite my comfort, deep inside I knew something was missing in my life. From listening to hours on end of personal development training, I knew I needed to learn how to manage people if I wanted to become a successful business owner, so I worked my butt off to get to a management position. Much to my surprise, I was told I was too young and had to wait a few years before I could become a manager. All I could think about was wondering if I was really about to do this routine for the next couple of years and hope that one day I would get promoted, without having any certainty of actually being given the promotion.

The lack of certainty about my future is what shifted my focus to my long-term vision. I asked myself if it would be okay to give up consistent money for the short-term in order to set myself up for later down the road. Time is valuable. If I decided to quit, I could start a business and force myself into a position where I had to manage people. But then I thought about the risk. How could I support myself? I did not even know what business I would want to start or how I would start it. But my heart told me I needed to do something. I knew I could grow so much more in two years if I applied what I learned, made a pivot, and got outside of my comfort zone.

On May 5, 2015, I gave my notice to quit the pipeline job, and it was the most amazing and scariest feeling ever. I was not the same person as when I had first started working at the company. Thanks to everything I had learned in my Chevy 2500 classroom, I had a whole new mindset that gave me the courage to move confidently in the direction of my dreams. I listened to my heart and intuition and decided to move back to Colorado. I had no idea what I was going to do, but it did not matter. One of my new core beliefs is that when you make a decision from your heart, God, the universe, or whatever you want to call it will acknowledge what you are doing and put the people and circumstances in front of you to help you succeed. Your only responsibility is to declare with certainty and courage what you are doing, take the first step, head in that direction, believe that it will happen no matter what, and pay attention to the people and events that begin to show up in your life.

On July 14, 2015, a bit over two months after my pivot, Pro Painters was born. I started my own interior/exterior home painting business without any experience. Since that decision to start my own business I have been applying everything I have learned and have been 'failing' my way to success. I have been through lots of ups and downs to make it a successful company. Every step along the way has been a challenging learning experience. I failed twenty times giving estimates to people before I ever got my first house to paint. When I painted my first house, I literally used YouTube to teach me how. I had never painted the outside of a house before, but it did not matter. I knew I wanted to build this company; I was teachable and willing to take the necessary risks.

The one pivot I made on May 5, 2015 has forever changed the direction of my life. At only 21 years old, I now have a very successful home painting business with a portfolio of satisfied customers, and plenty of referrals. Best of all, I am now a published author—something that so many people talk about, but never act toward achieving. All of this has happened because I learned that it is okay to be different, that you have to surround yourself with the right people, make things happen, get out of your comfort zone, and know when to pivot in a new direction.

LESSON SIX

BE GRATEFUL

*"When you are grateful, fear disappears,
and abundance appears."*
—Tony Robbins

In the short amount of time I have been alive, I have gained a lot of perspective about life. I grew up with all the necessities given to me. I always had my own room, food on the table, water to drink, a bathroom to use, but I never realized how much I took for granted until I moved to North Dakota to work with the pipeline company.

Moving to North Dakota was a total shock. I went from being a spoiled kid living in beautiful Colorado to living in a fifth wheel camper, sleeping on a couch for six months with no running water, and having to drive to a bathhouse just to use the bathroom. On top of that, the temperature was a chilling negative 30 degrees, not including wind-chill. I learned very fast how many things I was taking for granted. Looking back, I now also realize that If you are taking things for granted in one area of your life, you are most likely taking things for granted in all areas of your life.

Of all the lessons I learned, the importance of gratitude stands out the most. Since you can only focus on and feel one emotion at a time, why not let it be gratitude? No matter what your life looks like right now, you cannot feel anger and gratitude at the same time, nor can you feel resentment and gratitude at the same time. You get to choose the emotion that rules your life. Whatever you think, you feel. Whatever you feel determines the actions you take. Together your thoughts, feelings, and actions determine the life you live.

While living in my cold, sparse, North Dakota reality, I learned to give thanks for everything I had. Every morning I would wake up and hop in my truck and say to myself everything I was thankful for in about 10 minutes. It would be big things and small things.

I am so happy and thankful...
- ...I have warm clothes to wear.
- ...I have an amazing family.
- ...for waking up today.
- ...for having audio books to listen to.
- ...I have food to eat.
- ...I can support myself.
- ...for all God has given me.
- ...for all my amazing friends.
- ...that I have a car to drive
- ...that I have coaches and mentors.
- ...that I am free to be me.

After I started doing this day after day it was as if God said, *"Okay, Kyler, since you are grateful for all of this I will give you more."* All of this gratitude created mini-miracles in my life. I truly believe that having a grateful attitude is what made my transition back to Colorado so smooth, and it is why my business is so successful today.

Gratitude does not make your life challenges go away. Gratitude is not living with your head in the clouds and your feet in mid-air, hoping that things in your life get better. Rather, it is the belief that there is a universal power—what I call "God"— that will give you in abundance whatever you focus on. During times of difficulty, when you focus on gratitude, God will magnify the goodness in your life. When life is going well, and you remain grateful, God will extend those blessings in greater abundance.

Live with gratitude every day and your entire life will be a miracle.

Epilogue

I have come a long way since sitting in the college orientation at Arapahoe Community College. With a bit of courage and a high willingness to learn, my decision not to pursue a traditional college education has paid off handsomely. I am now in the process of becoming the man I have envisioned myself to become, and my dreams are becoming a reality.

Having now read my story, I challenge you to apply the five lessons in your own life so that you can begin to live your dreams.

Look at your life now. Do you have people who keep pulling you back down every time you tell them about a big change or big goal you want to accomplish, or are you surrounded by winners?

Think about your five closest friends. Do they share the same vision you have for your life? In five years, where will your life be if you keep hanging out with these same five people? Will you have more money? Better relationships? Greater success? Will you be healthier and happier? Or, will you be where you are right now, living the same life without any progress or improvement, and a few years older?

Who do you look up to? Who inspires you? Who challenges you always to learn and grow? A lot of people have crabs in their life, but they lack role models. They are being pulled down with no one to help pull them back up. Who can you reach out to that will help pull you up to where you want to go?

What is your vision for your life over the next 10 years? What is your comfort zone, and what do you need to do to get out of it? What are your strongest beliefs that will allow you to make a pivot in your life?

What talents do you have that you are not tapping into? What are your unique qualities—the things that make you different that you can build upon to create your dream life?

Who are the people that support you, and who are the crabs that drag you down?

What do you have to do to make things happen in your life? Where can you find mentors and coaches to help shape the life of your dreams?

Who and what are you grateful for? Think about the small things and the big things.

It is time to change your mindset. Live life as if everything is a learning experience. Use your failures to help you improve your thinking and propel you forward, toward your next adventure.

Get out of your daily routine. It is never easy to make changes when things are going well, but sometimes it is necessary to pursue your greater vision for your life.

Set goals for your life. Find your *why* that drives you—the one action motivator that will keep you moving forward, even when there are obstacles, distractions, or setbacks. Get an accountability partner and stay consistent.

You have what it takes. The only thing that is holding you back is that your current *why* is a *why not.* It is your self-doubt and the corresponding negative thoughts and beliefs that control your life.

Identify your limiting beliefs that are preventing you from stepping outside your comfort zone. If you want to change the results you are getting in your life, you must get outside your comfort zone so that you can grow to new heights.

Be adaptable. There are always going to be challenges to overcome. When you get out of your comfort zone, you step into your creative zone.

Do something different, and you will get different results. You have what it takes. Just believe in yourself and believe it is possible. It starts with you and taking that first step.

Be aware that the people that tend to pull you down the most are your closest friends and family. But the only reason they are pulling you down is that they do not believe it is possible for themselves. They do not want you to fail so they are doing what they can to "protect" you. Be grateful for their concern but still follow your heart and focus on yourself and what you want to accomplish.

Identify the naysayers in your life, the crabs that are trying to hold you back, and do what you can to minimize their impact on your life. In

EPILOGUE

their place, build a support group of people who enable you to realize your vision and support you on your journey.

Step back now. Find a quiet place and digest the thoughts and lessons of my story. You deserve to live the life of your dreams. It all begins with you.

***

Through sharing my story, I hope to have inspired or changed the life of at least one person. It is my long-term goal to help millions of people realize their full potential.

I am here to serve and help you. Reach out to me on social media. I am here as a tool to help you along your journey, so you can help inspire others, too.

I hope one day to shake your hand.

Thank you from the bottom of my heart for reading my story.

www.KylerGraff.com

Enjoyed this book?
Share the love...
Tweet, post, Insta...
#ThinkGenWhy
Facebook.com/ThinkGenWhy

Review on Amazon. Go to:
www.ThinkGenWhyBook.com

Acknowledgements

Without the help of all the amazing people in my life, this book would not be possible. There are so many people who have helped me and also pushed me outside of my comfort zone, which has allowed me to get to this present moment. I first have to say thank you to my parents. I know that I was not the easiest kid to raise, but you have done a great job. Thank you for all the support you have given me along my journey. Without you, I would not have been able to paint my first home.

I also need to give huge thanks to Colin Rudnick. Thank you for teaching me some of the basics of life. Living with you and Grandpa Mike were amazing times I cannot forget.

Thank you to Matteo. When you pushed me to hire subcontractors for my painting projects, instead of me doing the work, it changed everything. You inspired me and gave me the confidence to go out and make it happen.

Thank you to Tony Grebmeier. I am so grateful for all the knowledge and wisdom you have given me over the years. Thank you for always supporting me in everything I do. You have impacted my life tremendously.

Thank you to My DECA teacher, Mrs. Bryant. You always saw potential in me, and you motivated me to think outside of the box and be different. All the skills you taught me through marketing and DECA have helped me a lot in my life.

Thank you to Wes and Jo-Jo for supporting me with Pro Painters and helping grow my business to the next level.

Thank you to the members of the mastermind group I was a part of in 2016. You have all helped me grow into the man I am today. Thank you for all your guidance.

Thank you to all my lacrosse coaches growing up: Randy Hoffman, Jamie Monroe, Kevin Taggart, Ben Brenneman. You all taught me so much on the lacrosse field which I have been able to use in my life off the field. "Giving it your all when you're tired," "working together as a team."

Thank you to my grandparents on both sides of my family. I am blessed to call you family. Thank you for all your support

Thank you to my amazing girlfriend, Taylor. You are such an amazing person in my life. You supported me through all my crazy ideas. Thank you so much for being by my side figuring out this game called life. I think you influenced my decision to move back to Colorado. Not only was I able to move back and live my dreams, but that also meant seeing you a lot more.

A huge thank you to all my family, your love and support is greatly appreciated.

Thank you to my sisters. You both are amazing, and I am grateful to have both of you in my life.

Most of all, thank you to David Strauss, our coach and mentor, for helping this book become a reality. Your patience in working with all of us is truly appreciated.

BOOK TWO

Perfectly Imperfect

Four Lessons to Overcome a Cookie-Cutter Life

• Jesse Wright •

Prologue

*"Let the improvement of yourself keep you so busy
that you have no time to criticize others."*
—Roy T. Bennett, The Light in the Heart

How many people do you know who are smiling on the outside, but struggling on the inside?

For many people, genuine happiness is a real challenge. It certainly has been for me. I am an 18 year-old trying to make my way through life. I have had my fair share of mess-ups. I have done some things society would deem unacceptable. I have learned from my mistakes and managed to meet amazing people along the way. I have taken advantage of opportunities some people would never consider.

Yes, like lots of other kids, I had a rough childhood. There were a lot of ups and downs, especially when it came to money. My father had to work in other states to pay the bills for our family from time to time. There have been times when my parents had to go to food banks so we could have food on the table. One time my dog was sick and my family was so broke that we started a lemonade stand to make money to help pay for the vet bills. I have also seen my parents doing well, though it was not very often. However, one way or another, they always found a way to provide for our family.

Since money was always tight, my brother Eric and I were always on the grind, trying to earn money for our clothes, toys, electronics, and other silly things. Sometimes we had to help pay bills for our family instead of buying our own stuff.

Even though we lived in a nice neighborhood, we were living with a day-to-day mentality. With five kids to take care of, planning was very difficult for my parents. Everything was spur-of-the-moment and sporadic. Family dinners were planned the night of, and birthdays and holidays were usually planned a week before. It was a mentality of waking up and figuring out the day instead of planning the day in advance. This footloose lifestyle made me very rebellious.

I did a lot of crazy stuff growing up. Sometimes I got in trouble, sometimes not. Riding shirtless and shoeless, flying through the neighborhood on my orange Mongoose bike was a regular experience. This reckless mindset ended soon after running into the back of a parked car and getting all scraped up. I was more of an experiential learner and this also reflected in my academics.

I attended Mountain Vista High School where I tapped into my love for sports. After playing football freshman year and continuously getting hurt, I had to take a year off to recover. During my junior year, I found my passion when I joined the varsity cheerleading team. This also presented enormous challenges. I had to learn a lot of different techniques in a short period which put my physical and mental agility to the test.

I had to pick up cheer quickly, and when I did, I took it to the next level: all-star cheerleading. From there I learned how to be very coachable as well as how to accept constructive criticism. Joining a new sport and having to learn everything very quickly was a challenging process that resulted in me becoming very teachable, and it strengthened my leadership and people skills.

Like many teenagers, despite seeming happy on the outside, I was struggling on the inside. I never fit in. I never felt accepted. Depression followed me through high school. Though I was attending a prominent High School, I ended up not graduating due to low self-esteem. I found myself in an educational system that did not recognize or was unable to tap into my native genius, and so I saw no reason to finish.

While in school I realized that the educational system treats everyone the same, even though they are not. Everyone learns differently and at their own pace, but the *system* does not adapt to those differences.

How crazy would it be if we expected every animal in the animal kingdom to be able to climb a tree? Well, what about that fish? Or that elephant? Or even the giraffe? They all have their own special characteristics and adaptations. The fish can breathe underwater. It is cold-blooded and can live in conditions unimaginable to a warm-blooded lion. Elephants have an amazing memory. They have a mental map of every water hole within miles. The main purpose of a giraffe's neck was the adaptation of not being able to climb a tree. These are qualities that a monkey or mountain lion do not have. My teachers were expecting me to climb a tree when I was a bird that could just soar to the top.

> *"Everybody is a genius. But if you judge a fish by its ability to climb a tree, it will live its whole life believing that it is stupid."*
> — Einstein

I was never good enough academically because I was never taught the way I like to learn. Failing nearly every class after putting hundreds of hours of effort into them was a very heavy burden to carry in my mid-teens that led to me constantly cutting class. After finishing my junior year, I ended up dropping out. Nonetheless, I never gave up on myself. My "failure" in the school environment became the catalyst for me to discover the path of self-help and personal development.

The academic system prepares students for a cookie-cutter life:
- Wake up, get ready, eat food, drive to work
- Work from 9am to 5pm
- Spend time with family and friends
- Get to sleep
- Rinse and repeat

Living a "one-size-fits-all" cookie-cutter lifestyle was the exact opposite of my personality and was not my destiny. My choices and challenges led me to read books and go to seminars which taught me how to be an independent thinker and develop business and leadership skills that were not taught in school. I quickly came to realize that many of the most successful people never finished an advanced education, and some never finished their basic education, but instead, they became thought leaders and entrepreneurs.

Through all my independent learning, I tapped into a new way of thinking that I wish had been taught in school because it makes sense to me, and I love it. Even though I am still young, I have tapped into five valuable lessons which guide my actions and give me the clarity to make good decisions. I live by these lessons every day, and they keep my life perfectly imperfect.

1) Have the courage to be yourself
2) Change your mindset, change your life
3) Raise your people standards
4) Be the leader of your own life
5) Develop a winning philosophy

LESSON ONE

Have the Courage To Be Yourself

*"Be who you are and say what you feel,
because those who mind don't matter,
and those who matter don't mind."*
— Dr. Seuss

Do you have the courage to be yourself? When you hang out with different people do you change who you are so they will like you, or are you always the same person?

If you are the type of person who is always adapting your personality so you can fit in, you may want to do what I did and follow these three suggestions for getting to know yourself so that you can feel comfortable in your own skin.

- Get clear about who you are
- Get out of your comfort zone
- Walk away from negativity

GET CLEAR ABOUT WHO YOU ARE

While I was in school, I was in a continuous tug-of-war between my desire to be liked and accepted by others and feeling comfortable with who I am. I struggled pretty hard with my identity, which means I never knew where I fit in amongst my friends. I adapted to my different social groups because I wanted to be accepted, but it always left me feeling empty inside. Shortly after dropping out of high school I felt the weight of that emptiness fall off my shoulders. I no longer had to try and meet other people's expectations, but instead had the time to begin figuring out who I am and what I want.

Even though I got some crap from people for dropping out of high school, I knew it was the best thing for me. Trying to fit into the cookie-cutter game plan was suffocating me and fueling my depression. I was shrinking instead of growing.

When you are dealing with low self-esteem, sometimes you have to take massive action that goes against all the norms and everything you were taught to believe in order to overcome those destructive feelings. That is what it took for me. I had to put my courage to the test so I could get clear about who I am, and I am glad I did.

Some people believe that the need for courage is limited to going after what you want in life. Sometimes, as it was for me, it takes courage to break away from what you *do not* want so that you can step into the unknown and figure out what you do want. The unknown that I was stepping into was discovering what is important to me so I could become the best version of me. The funny thing is, it took more courage for me to deal with the stress and expectations of school than it did to leap into the uncertainty of dropping out of school.

GET OUT OF YOUR COMFORT ZONE

Even though I was unhappy in school, it was an environment that I was familiar with. I was comfortably uncomfortable. But when I reached that point of complete frustration and made the decision not to return, it was partly because I realized that living in a comfort zone was not taking me to the next level of the life I wanted to live, and it was preventing me from truly discovering who I am.

Living where you are comfortable and never challenging yourself—even if it is painful—is very disempowering. Living behind the wall that you built to protect yourself not only separates you from the pain you are fearful of experiencing; it also separates you from experiencing your true, authentic self and shields you from the love and opportunity that is coming your way.

Having the courage to be yourself goes way deeper than getting out of your comfort zone. Being courageous is also learning to love and accept yourself, and to be accepting of change. It is taking that change and wrapping your hand around it and sprinting in a new direction—full speed ahead. It is putting yourself out there and being uncomfortable in new situations that yesterday you could not or would not have handled. Being courageous is experiencing new things that you are unaware of so that you can get to the unfamiliar place where you want to be—a place you are passionate about and want to experience because it is important to you.

There are a lot of people who do not realize that they are in a comfort zone until something disrupts their life and they have to start thinking differently and doing things differently. This disruption can happen when someone becomes injured, the death of someone you love, loss of a career or relationship, or any other type of situation which shocks your reality. There are also people who have been doing the same thing throughout their life and continuously getting the same results, but when the time comes and their life must change, they think that they can live and act in the same way and get a different outcome. A lot of people do this. They want their life to change as long as they do not have to do anything any differently. This type of thinking is insanity and will never lead you to discover who you are.

A big part of the reason people become stuck in a comfort zone is that our culture is all about conformity. We are trained to think that the cookie-cutter way is the only way to do things. But in reality, there is not just one way to do things. If you really want to, you can create your own path that is unlike anyone else's.

Some people will stay in their comfort zone throughout their life and will not achieve anything extraordinary. They will be the same person year after year. But for those people who feel the need to scratch the itch of curiosity and adventure, breaking free from conformity is the only option.

WALK AWAY FROM NEGATIVITY

The people with the courage to chart their own path understand that the direction of their life is a choice. Their happiness begins with the courage to walk away from negativity, and they surround themselves with uplifting people who will help them improve their life. They realize that just because someone is conditioned to believe that they can only be happy by living in a *safe* zone does not mean that their belief is true. Being safe can also be a trap that prevents people from experiencing the rewards of living with courage and taking risks.

When I took that leap of faith and dropped out of school, I walked away from the *comfort zone* lie and trap. I took on the challenge of overcoming my negativity and the negativity of the people in the cookie-cutter system that I previously allowed to affect my thinking. My inner conversation changed from depression to becoming the cheerleader for my own life. Here were my new thoughts:

Get out and thrive. Stop surviving. Take that leap of faith. Believe in yourself. If you fail, get your ass back up and go back to work. When you begin to feel low and disempowered, try something different. Do not mope around and get lost in more negative thoughts. Go on a walk, go for a hike, drive your car around the city or mountains. Surround yourself with giraffes—with confident people and leaders who will help you reach your potential. Get up and do something different so you can achieve the results you have been searching for.

LESSON TWO

CHANGE YOUR MINDSET, CHANGE YOUR LIFE

"A person's outlook on life colors their interpretation of specific events. Human beings' behavioral and thinking patterns enable people to thrive or cause them to live in despondency and despair."
— *Kilroy J. Oldster,* Dead Toad Scrolls

Some people believe that it is your life experiences that form you into who you are. There are others who believe your choice about what those experiences mean shapes you.

Two people can have the same experience and completely different outcomes because they see the experience differently, and they ask different questions. One person can learn a lesson from a difficult experience, and the other can blame people and situations, and become a victim. The people who learn have a mindset that every experience has its lesson, and they ask themselves questions to uncover those lessons. They believe that you can change your life by changing your beliefs about past experiences. When you change your mindset, you change your life.

My life experiences have formed me into who I am because I learned how to change my mindset. I have chosen to find the positive lesson in all that I experience. If it were not for my choice to focus on what I can learn from my experiences, I would never have been able to step up and take responsibility for my life.

My first glimpse into the benefits of changing how you think occurred in middle school when I discovered six things that you need to do to change your mindset.

1) Ask a different question
2) Create and test a new theory
3) Raise your people standards
4) Become a team player
5) Fail your way to success
6) Stamp out hesitation

ASK A DIFFERENT QUESTION

When I was in middle school, I did not understand how to deal with people. I would say things, and in my mind, they would seem 100% correct. However, when the words came out of my mouth, they would sound incredibly rude. Even though I was not trying to be rude, it came across that way due to how I worded what I had said. I did not understand that I could have said what I needed to say without coming across in a negative way.

One day, as I watched and listened to someone get a positive reaction out of a negative situation, I thought about it for a while and then asked myself a question.

"What can I say or do differently?"

When I asked myself that one simple question, I identified my problem, and the solution came to me almost instantly. Whenever I did not get the reaction I wanted, it was because I was putting someone in a bad position. I was not looking at things from the other person's point of view, only from mine. I was so caught up in what I wanted to say, or things I wanted to do, that I could not even see things from the other person's perspective. I never took the time to sit back and just think about them and how what I might have said could have been hurtful, or what I might have done that could have been perceived differently. When I realized this, I decided to create a new theory about how to talk with people, and I put the theory to the test.

CREATE AND TEST A NEW THEORY

Given my new and fresh view of how to think from another person's point of view, I developed a new theory for myself.

If you want to get something from other people or life, you also have to be a giver.

With this new idea, I made a list of all the things I wanted, and then thought about what I would normally do or say to get those things. I put my thoughts in writing which gave me a better picture of how I would normally approach things. I noticed how some of what I had written could be perceived as being rude or selfish, so I changed things up a little. I tweaked what I had to say so that when I talked with people, I showed interest in them, too. Then, I tested my new speaking style.

One day I needed a ride to work. Instead of just asking a friend for a ride, I also asked them if they needed help with anything. My new theory worked great. I was no longer perceived as being rude or selfish. This was not shallow, manipulative horse-trading to get what I wanted. I learned that if you show genuine interest in people and their needs, they will do the same for you. People love to give to people who make them feel good.

RAISE YOUR STANDARDS

When I learned that in order to get you have to give, it occurred to me that it is easier to get what you want if you surround yourself with the right people and you tap into resources to help improve your life.

I applied this lesson by raising my standards. I became clear about the lifestyle I wanted to create for myself, and then developed a competitive, winning mindset that allowed me to get what I wanted by focusing on how to give value to others. I also started surrounding myself with successful people who had the same mindset that I wanted so that I could learn from them, and give value to them, in return.

One of the things I learned by observing successful people is that they keep track of their progress on a regular basis. Doing this makes sense. How else would you know if you are making good decisions if you do not measure the outcome of your choices? I started doing this for my life. Instead of comparing myself and my progress to other people, I began to compare myself to who I was yesterday. If I am the same person today that I was yesterday, then I have failed my day. This may seem harsh, but if I am truly committed to raising my standards, I have to challenge myself based on my results, not someone else's.

This new approach to life—raising my standards—gave me a glimpse into how I could create the lifestyle that I hungered for. The more I challenged myself to improve, the more connected I felt to my new way of thinking. My positive results were reinforcing my new attitude toward life and helping me to achieve greater results than I had previously accomplished.

Raising your standards does not just help you to learn and grow, it also adds value to other people's lives because they get the benefits of the effects of your positive, uplifting attitude. Having high standards also adds to the ability to find quick solutions to problems so that you can take immediate action toward that solution. This happens because instead of making trial-by-error decisions, you follow the advice of people who have the results and success that you want. When I learned that in order to *get* you have to *give*, it occurred to me that it is easier to get what you want if you surround yourself with the right people and you tap into resources to help you improve your life.

So, what did I do? I raised my standards. I became clear about the lifestyle I want to create for myself, and then developed a competitive, winning mindset that allowed me to get what I want by focusing on how to give value to others. I started surrounding myself with people who had the same winning mindset I wanted so that I could learn from them.

BECOME A TEAM PLAYER

Not too long ago, when I had just turned 18 and the summer was coming to a wrap, I found an opportunity to develop my leadership and team-player skills. I got involved in a business with three other guys, helping to run a warehouse that was used to fulfill Amazon.com online sales. We would buy these massive truckloads of *stuff* and break it down into individual items and resell them on Amazon.com.

I had a crew of about nine that I worked with on a daily basis. My job was not only to make sure all the work got done, but also to control the mental and emotional energy of the room so that everyone could work in the best environment as possible, while at the same time making sure that the warehouse was running efficiently. I was the oil for this machine. I would apply myself to the areas where there was the most tension and release the tension to make things run as smoothly as possible. I made sure people were doing what they were supposed to do, and if they were not, I would put myself into those gaps and fill them.

It may not seem like a tough job, but it was a big responsibility having to always be alert and willing to do different things at different times. It required me to constantly be on my toes and aware of everything that was going on. For some people this may have been an easy job, but with my previous failures in communication, this team-player approach would not have been possible had I not learned from my earlier mistakes.

FAIL YOUR WAY TO SUCCESS

When I use the word *failure* or *failed,* I do not mean it literally. I do not think it is possible to fail if you are always learning. I see failure as a pause instead of a stopping point. It is okay to fail. It is okay to fail hard. It is okay to fall on your ass every once in a while. According to my new standards, it is not okay to stay on your ass. It is not okay to live your life in a low state. I believe you were put on this earth to overcome your fears and to thrive. If you want to thrive, you have to be willing to fail your way to success. You have to be willing to take new risks, try new things, and learn from your failures. Most importantly, you have to commit to facing and overcoming your fears.

It has been said that humans are born with only two innate fears—the fear of falling and the fear of loud sounds. If this is true, why is it that we live and die with hundreds of fears? The answer is obvious. We are taught fears through our environment as we grow up, and we also learn them from TV and movies.

Most of us were raised by people with good intentions who want to keep us safe. Unknowingly by being overprotective they are teaching us to be afraid of risk or danger instead of teaching us how to calculate risk and learn from failures. TV and movies are masterful at reinforcing our fears by putting them right in our face with full sound and visual effects.

Our fears seem real, but they are mostly made up in our head, and a lot of them do not make any sense when you think about them. For example, with the fear of failure, most people are actually afraid of being judged by others. They believe that no one will like them, or they will lose friends or family if they fail, so they create a story in their mind of why they should not even take the risk.

Part of growing up is realizing that sometimes you have to face your fears and put yourself into an uncomfortable position so that you can make your life better. If you were a jackrabbit, you would sometimes have to fight a rattlesnake out in the desert. The rabbit is aware of the dangers but goes out and lives its life anyway. It is survival. How are you going to live your life to the fullest if you are always afraid of the rattlesnakes? Be like a rabbit. Take action despite your fears.

I am going to call out my brother Eric. That man is afraid of sharks, and he has only been to the ocean four times. We all do it. We all have fears that seem irrational. Mine is the fear of not being a good father and not being able to provide and supply for my family. How is that even relevant to me? I am 18, and I do not even have a kid, nor am I planning on having one anytime soon. But I created that fear because not being able to provide enough for my family is a scary thought. It would be highly important to me to be able to meet the financial needs of my family, and that is one place I definitely would not want to fail.

Failing your way to success is a choice, and so is facing your fears. Every time you face a fear, you become more confident and secure, which makes it easier to face a similar situation the next time it shows up. When you are ready to face your fears, ask yourself these three questions.

- What would your life be like if you overcame your fears?
- What would you do differently?
- What would you accomplish?

STAMP OUT HESITATION

We all have those moments when we take a risk and it completely advances our life. My risk and leap of faith was competitive cheerleading. It all started around my junior year. My good friend Ryan Miller, one of the authors of this book, helped me to get signed up into high school cheer. One day Ryan came over to me he asked, *"Jesse, what sports or athletic activities are you thinking about doing this year?"* Having put no thought into that, I said, *"Probably nothing."*

The truth is, I was too afraid to do another sport because I did not want to get hurt over and over again. It just did not sound fun, comforting an injury every week. All I could think about after playing tackle football and hurting my hip in track was injuries. I had created this completely false reality in my brain about the injuries. They were not as frequent as I thought them out to be, and they were not as severe as I had perceived them to be. So, what was my issue? As I thought this through in my mind, trying to figure out what was holding me back, Ryan asked the next question. *"Would you be willing to look into cheer?"* And that's when all the thoughts began: Girls, flips, GIRLS, throwing girls, catching girls—you get it. You can guess what my answer was. *"Sure, I'll give it a shot, and if I like it, I will stick with it."*

Over the next few weeks I got out of my comfort zone and learned an entirely new set of skills. It started with back flips. I lived in a neighborhood with two awesome families that combined their backyards. They had a trampoline that I would regularly bounce on. I started learning my back flips on that. I tried several different times, and every time
I would land on my knees. Feeling determined to figure out how to do a flip, late one night I met Ryan at a trampoline place down the road. Ryan got me set up by putting one hand on my lower back and his other hand right

behind my knees to help guide my legs over my head during mid-flight. We kept doing that until I got it down. After learning a standing back flip in an hour or so, it was time to learn it on the ground.

The next day, Ryan came over to my house and we went out onto the front lawn. He spotted me again. I got set up. Ryan was to my right and was all set and ready. As usual, I sat back into a squat, threw my hands up in the air as I simultaneously stood up and set myself into the flip by jumping up and backward. All I had to do next was just pull my feet up and act like I was bringing my knees over my head. That is where it all went wrong. I bailed out of my flip. Why? Nothing was different. I was not going to fall, nor was I afraid to fall. So why would I think I could not do it? It was because the feeling of the ground changed. I bailed out of my flip because the grass felt less forgiving than the trampoline. I doubted my abilities and became afraid that I would not be able to make it around into a full flip. I had thought about it so much that I started creating a self-defeating belief in my mind—a fake reality of the potential outcome of my back flip. I did not think I could make it around, so I gave up. Once I launched my flip, I was 90% done. All I had to do was finish flipping and land on my feet, which is not hard when you have a spot. But I gave up. Ryan checked me at that moment. He encouraged me and told me that I knew I could do it and asked why I was not doing it. He asked what I was even afraid of. I had no excuse, so I said, *"Nothing."* I got back up and did it. I did it again the second try.

After my second successful flip, I realized that all of my fears were mental. If they were not mental, I would not have even been able to do a flip the second time. It was fearful anticipation about the flip that caused me to miss my first one. When I doubted myself, it led me to busting and smacking down on the grass. When I had a spot, I felt safer.

Your mind can do unimaginable things. It can block your actions based on false fears, or it can empower you to achieve great things based on confident beliefs. The accomplishments come if you allow yourself to take action without letting fear and doubt get in the way. The lesson learned is simple.

Stamp out hesitation before it turns into fear.

LESSON THREE

BE THE LEADER OF YOUR OWN LIFE

*"It's only after you've stepped outside your comfort zone
that you begin to change, grow, and transform."*
— Roy T. Bennett

No one can live your life for you, and no one can die for you. You have to be the leader of your own life or you will become the builder of someone else's dreams. When I chose to abandon the one-size-fits-all mentality and become my own leader, I began to follow five benchmarks of leadership.

1) Be humble
2) Practice patience
3) Become self-aware
4) Be respectful
5) Be resourceful

BE HUMBLE

Everyone wants to feel good about themselves, to be liked by others, and to live their dreams. There is no doubt that it takes confidence to make things happen in your life, but have you ever met someone who is good at what they do, but they are confident to the point of being arrogant? When they talk, they are so full of themselves, you think to yourself, *"Damn, that guy is in love with himself. Get a room for yourself, buddy."* Not only is it annoying to hear someone with a self-inflated ego talk about themselves, there is also no fun in listening to someone who is so infatuated with themselves that it stinks up the whole room.

People who are arrogant are like the wizard in the film, *The Wizard of Oz*. They are a small person hiding behind a curtain, speaking into a microphone. They seem big and strong, but they are very unsure of themselves, so they find a way to make themselves look good and gain acceptance, but they are actually masking their deeper insecurities.

Someone who is confident knows that they are good at something, but they are not insecure, so they do not have to boast about themselves to be liked by others. They can build their confidence in other areas of life because they have a high willingness to learn, they are coachable, and are willing to set priorities. They allow their accomplishments to be their source of validation instead of being validated by the approval of others.

There is a higher level of confidence that is admired. People who are confident and humble are the ones who truly understand life. Humility is when you are free of pride and arrogance. People who are humble take full responsibility for their lives, they readily admit their mistakes and forgive easily. Their focus is shifted outward towards other people rather than upon themselves. They tend to be grateful, considerate of others, and recognize other people's potential and strengths. They are usually the ones who will help other people overcome their weakness so that they can better themselves.

Being humble is a must when it comes to being the leader of your own life. You have to know when you are good at something, when you have something to learn, and what your gifts are that you can use to help others.

PRACTICE PATIENCE

Anyone who takes on the responsibility of being the leader of their own life has learned how to practice patience. I got an early start to learning patience.

As a kid, I hardly ever got anything I wanted. Having four other siblings almost guaranteed that someone would need something at that exact moment that I wanted something, and so I always found myself setting my wants aside. If I broke something of my own, it would take months to get something new. Sometimes it would never get replaced because it was not a priority.

Being the second youngest of five also gave me a thick skin. It taught me to let go of what people say and do and not to take things personally.

I was always getting picked on by my older siblings. This forced me to grow up quickly and become much more mature for my age.

My whole childhood was about patience because there was never any certainty about when things would happen, and it took a lot of patience to tolerate the constant abuse of my siblings. From these challenges, I realized that change does not happen overnight and that
I have to learn how to establish boundaries of what is and is not acceptable in my life and to set priorities.

BECOME SELF-AWARE

One of the most important steps to take when becoming the leader of your own life is to become self-aware. You need to know what is going on in your life and be tuned into the things that are happening around you. It starts with having an honest conversation with yourself about where you are in your life right now, and asking yourself some key questions. Are you healthy? Do you feel a sense of worth and fulfillment? Does your life have a purpose? Is everything going smoothly and do you feel like you are on track to living your dreams, or do you feel held back by your fears and the need to fit in and be accepted by others?

Self-awareness is key. Not only do you need to be aware of the conditions of your life, but you also need to be aware of the primary emotions with which you are living. Your emotions determine the choices you make. If you are living in a constant state of stress or overwhelm, you will make different choices than if you feel relaxed, confident, and courageous.

Most people allow their emotions to be determined by their experiences. For example, if they are low on money they feel broke. They are allowing a financial condition to affect their emotions, not realizing that if you feel broke, you will prevent yourself from turning into situations that will help you prosper. When you are self-aware, you know how to choose the emotions that will help you manage your life, and how to get into those emotional states quickly. If you do not know how to manage your emotions or how to communicate with yourself about how you are feeling, then you will not be able to use your emotions to your advantage. Either you use your emotions, or they use you.

Being the leader of your own life also means knowing how to impact others with your emotions. People can be very intuitive when it comes to the way you say things, and they can sense emotions by the way you speak and through your body language. If you cannot talk about the way you feel with sincerity, how are you ever going to come across as being genuine? As I learned through my own experience, you need to be aware of how you communicate with others and whether or not you are likable and believable.

Instead of being self-aware, a lot of people are self-conscious. They are unsure of themselves, so they do not take a leadership role in their own life. They are afraid to initiate conversations with other people, especially strangers, out of fear of being judged. Because of this, they are missing out on a lot of life because most opportunities come from people you meet and reach out to during your daily life.

People who are self-conscious are in a double-bind. Many of them want to feel confident and be the leader of their own lives, but their beliefs limit them from having the conversations and meeting the people who will help them to take their life to the next level.

BE RESPECTFUL

To be the leader of your own life you have to develop habits of respect. Developing respect for yourself and others goes hand-in-hand with becoming self-aware. For me, respect is a feeling of admiration for someone based on the result of their achievements, or their qualities and abilities that set them apart from others. Self-respect is when you recognize your worth and achievements, and you treat yourself the way you would want to be treated by others. This includes surrounding yourself with the right people who are on the same life path as you.

If someone does not like or respect themselves, it shows up in how they treat others. Have you ever had the experience of someone walking all over you or taking advantage of you? What do you do to stop that or keep that from happening? You cannot stop others from treating you disrespectfully, but when this happens, you can ask yourself if it is just them and their mentality, or did you do something to trigger their abuse?

Through the years, I have learned a very valuable lesson: respect is earned. Some people, out of their arrogance, demand respect, but you cannot walk around demanding people to like you or treat you a certain way if they do not see you that way. If someone is treating you poorly and it is undeserved, do what you can to distance yourself from them. Part of self-respect is choosing the type of people you allow into your life.

If there were a respect-o-meter that measured how much you respect yourself and others, or how much you are respected, where would you be on a scale of 1 to 10?

Here are a few questions that will help you think about how you treat yourself and other people.

- What are you doing to make people want to look up to you?
- What about you is likable?
- How well do you treat others?
- What do you do to love and respect yourself?
- How do you think other people describe you when talking to their friends?
- Do people perceive you as being authentic?
- Have you set up any boundaries to protect yourself from negative or disruptive people?
- If people push your boundaries, what steps do you take to avoid that from happening again?

These are all very important questions to ask yourself because most people can see through insincerity. If you are truly committed to being the leader of your own life, set yourself up with a reliable and likable image. Brand yourself in your own way, and people will have no option but to love you. The more you respect and love yourself the more you are going to receive that love and respect from other people. Never settle for anything less than the way you deserve to be treated. Get away from toxic people and surround yourself with anyone who loves you for who you are. Respect yourself enough to put yourself into empowering positions.

When I dropped out of school, it was because I felt like the entire school system disrespected my individuality and I could not find a way to fit in and make things work. Looking back, even though it was a tough choice, that was one of my first big steps in respecting myself. I chose not to conform and instead to transform into being the leader of my own life.

BE RESOURCEFUL

There is no more valuable trait to develop in the pursuit of taking a leadership role in your own life than that of being resourceful. Being resourceful is a mindset that does not see limits or obstacles. When you are resourceful, you do not care what you do or do not have because you know that when you are committed to your outcome, you will find a way to make it happen or create your own path.

Most often people think of resources as money or tangible objects, but the greatest and most valuable resources are time, people, and your imagination.

Close your eyes and think about how different your life would be if you did not have many of the luxuries of life; the convenience of eating out, watching TV, cell phones, cars, and technology. What about indoor running water? Hot water? A refrigerator? Toilet paper? Heating and air conditioning? Automobile? None of these would exist if their inventors were not resourceful. They came up with an idea, used their imaginations, and connected with people to help make all of them become a reality. They did not know how they were going to do it, but they stayed focused, tapped into their resources, failed a few times, and eventually succeeded.

Now let us put this into the human perspective. If people are a resource, what type of people would you want in your life? What would happen to your life if you surrounded yourself with people who think negatively or have a horrible outlook on life or people who act hopeless and helpless? Unless you had a much stronger mindset than them, you might become negative, hopeless, and helpless, too. What if you only allowed people into your life who were confident and successful, and continuously encouraging you? How much better would that be?

The people in your life either cause you to shrivel up and weaken, or to blossom, learn, and grow. You would not go to a pastor for math help. You would want to go to the best person who knows how to teach math. Look at where you are right now and where you want to go with your life. Do you have the right people resources lined up who are going to help you get the results you are looking for? Who do you have in your life that you can rely on to help you get to the next level? You want at least one of these people in every big aspect of your life. If you do not yet have those people lined up, what do you need to do to find them? More importantly, are there any people who you may want to shed from your life? One rotten apple can spoil the batch.

Each of these five benchmarks of leadership are starting points for becoming the leader of your own life. The most important step is the first step. Have an honest conversation with yourself about your life, and move forward from there.

LESSON FOUR

DEVELOP A WINNING PHILOSOPHY

"Strength does not come from winning. Your struggles develop your strengths. When you go through hardships and decide not to surrender, that is strength."
—*Arnold Schwarzenegger*

Everyone has a philosophy of life. Some follow a religion, others create their own belief systems, and some people just go with the flow. Some people believe the earth is flat and others believe the moon is a hollow satellite put into orbit by aliens.

Everyone has a reason to believe what they believe. Some people are aggro about their beliefs, and some are very casual or wishy-washy. Some people have a loser philosophy and see themselves as victims, while others have a champion philosophy and see themselves as always winning.

In the short time that I have been alive, I have observed that the most successful people have a winning philosophy that includes five anchor beliefs which keep them in a winner's mindset. These five anchors give them the power to persist when faced with adversity, and the stamina to never give up.

- Don't worry about what other people think
- Don't let people get in the way of your passions
- Don't give up
- Don't help the butterfly
- Be grateful

DON'T WORRY ABOUT WHAT OTHER PEOPLE THINK

There are some things that are out of your control and some things that you cannot change. One of those things is people's perception of you. We all aspire to be liked and loved by others, but that is just not realistic. You cannot please everyone, and if you try to, you will be wearing so many different masks that you will forget who you are. The only person you truly need to please is yourself. If you set standards for yourself of what is and is not acceptable, and you live up to those standards, then you are setting yourself up to win.

Most successful people do not care about what others think about them. They are not looking for the validation of others. This does not mean that they are reckless with their actions. It only means that their self-perception is their highest priority and the driving force behind their decisions. They know what they want, they know what they believe, and they go for it.

Where do you fit into this picture? When you believe in something, is it when it is trendy and relevant, or are you unwavering and constant? Would you back your beliefs when proven wrong just to be right, or are you adaptable to new ideas? I have noticed that a lot of people in my generation will stick to a belief, even after being proven wrong, because their identity is wrapped up in what they believe. They are afraid to change or are concerned that they may lose their friends if they started to think differently, so they hold onto an idea that has no footing.

A lot of people my age still believe Pluto is a planet even though its classification was changed and is now considered a dwarf planet. Silly, right? But that is what they were trained to think. They were taught in school that it is a planet, and then six years later they are told differently and expected just to forget what was originally taught. But it doesn't work that easily. For you to let go of a belief, you have to accept that the person or teacher you were learning from was wrong. If they were wrong about one thing, what else were they wrong about? Changing one belief sets off an entire chain of events which can be too much for some people to handle, so they just hang onto old beliefs because they are safe.

What beliefs are you holding onto that is wrong or no longer true? Are you holding onto them out of laziness or are you afraid of what may happen if you start to think differently? Do you have any strong beliefs that you keep to yourself because you are afraid of what other people may think? I believe in Jesus, the son of God, as my savior. I believe we are God's children. I follow God's commandments to the best of my abilities. I go to church when I can, and I am passionate about my beliefs. Some people are afraid to show their passion, but they should not be. You have to be true to yourself. If your beliefs make sense to you and they keep you living an honest life with integrity, then you should wear them with pride and humility.

It does not matter what other people think of you. What matters is that when you look in the mirror, you can feel good about who you are and what you are doing, and never at the expense of harming others.

The need for acceptance is one of our top priorities while we are young. The way we dress, talk, eat, speak, and the activities we participate in are all driven by our need for acceptance. A lot of the stereotypes that we try and fall into are driven by TV, movies, and music. If we do not figure out who we are at a young age, our insecurities will carry into our adulthood and translate into low self-esteem, bad relationships, addictions, or other mental or emotional challenges.

Have you ever noticed the type of people that try way too hard? Everything they do is for attention. I like to call them the *sheep people* or the *sheeple* because they are like sheep. They are followers, not leaders, and will do anything to fit in. They want to be like everyone else so that they will be liked. Different is too scary or unpredictable. These people are so caught up in what everyone else thinks about them that they do not even take the time to figure out what is important to them.

If you are a *sheeple,* step back and find a way to develop some courage so that you can get over your need to be liked and validated by everyone else. Find something to believe in, something to stand for that is going to better your life—something that gets you excited and internally motivated. Whether it is religion, sports, adventures, becoming a chef, or anything else that makes you smile and is close to your heart, find something that can challenge you in a healthy way so that you can build your self-esteem and begin to change your life. For me, I have positive reminders, and I have constant positive reinforcement from the people around me. I have set myself up with a brotherhood of like-minded people that always have my back and hold me accountable to everything.

If you are truly committed to not caring what other people think about you, then it is crucial to have people around you who keep you on track and focused on continuously building your self-esteem and staying on the path that you have paved for yourself. Surround yourself with winners, with people who care about the way you think about yourself. If you do not have people around you supporting what you are doing, then you are setting yourself up to be overcome and influenced by people with negative attitudes who could potentially bring you down.

Your five closest friends are the most important decision you can make because they will determine where you go in life. If you are hanging out with people that are unable to contribute to your growth, you will not be able to move to the next level. As Joel Osteen says:

> "If you are spending time with the wrong people,
> you will never see the right ones."

DON'T LET PEOPLE GET IN THE WAY OF YOUR PASSIONS

Have you ever let yourself lose thinking about your dreams? Do you wish you could just live in a dream that you have had?

Imagine the perfect world. Imagine what you would be doing if nothing mattered and you could just do anything and everything. Are you the type that would want to be walking along the shoreline of the beach with the nice calm breeze on your skin and the warm sand filling in the cracks between your toes? The sun gently radiating onto your skin as it sets and turns the sky a nice orange and blood red color. The sound of the waves rumbling in the background as your kids are running in and out of the water, with an occasional smack from a hit from the volleyball game going on down by the lifeguard hut.

Now tell me why you cannot have that or any other dream. Tell me why you cannot have whatever dreams and aspirations you have been searching for in life. If it was not obtainable then why does it even exist in your mind in the first place? If you can see it in your mind, it has the potential to become your reality.

Most people never live their dreams because they let other people get in the way of their passions. They let other people's opinions affect them, or they get distracted by life events. Life happens. Things come up which can push you off course from your dreams, but it is up to you to find your way back to the path of your choosing. If you do not find your way back, then you will drift away until it seems too far, and you will settle for what was easy.

Living your passions is not always easy. There is plenty of reasons to divert your attention somewhere else, but think about this: when your life nears its end and you have a chance to look back, do you want to look back with regret, or celebrate the fact that you had the courage and willpower to stay the course and create your reality?

People are going to get in your way along the way. It is life. As the famous motivational speaker, Les Brown says:

"They're either on the way or in the way."

This quote is powerful for me. There are only two types of people in your life—the people that are there for you or the people who slow you down and stop you along the way. If you are spending your time with people that are always in the way, do whatever you can to get them out of the way so that you can make room for new people who will help your passions become a reality.

DON'T GIVE UP

Once you get the people who are holding you back out of the way, make sure that you do not get in your own way. You alone can convince yourself to quit or to make it past the finish line of your dreams.

When life keeps hammering you with problem after problem, like a ship battered by waves in a ferocious storm, how are you going to react? Are you going to resolve the problem and get right to the solution, or hem-and-haw, hoping the problem goes away? Either one is a choice, each with its respective destiny.

A lot of people will have a dream, a burning passion for doing something, and they will get started, but just as things get hard, they quit. They cannot make it through the storm because they are afraid to feel pain. They are scared of pain. But what is the pain they are afraid of? Is it the pain of change? The fear of losing what is important to them? Is it the pain of uncertainty, or the fear of failure? Is pain a bad thing?

For some people, pain is a giant wall, and they see no way around it. For others, pain is a source of motivation. When the pain becomes strong enough, it becomes powerful leverage that forces them to break past any barriers and catapults them toward their dreams. Some of the most successful people come from the most horrible and painful backgrounds. For them, rock bottom is the place upon which they built the foundation for their future.

When I dropped out of school, I was not giving up. That was the day that I declared my independence and took responsibility for my own life. I had to get away from all the mental and emotional pressure of trying to conform. The sense of relief afterward was confirmation that I had made the right choice.

Whether or not you give up on something in life has everything to do with the way you think. Have you ever had a headache and you just sat there thinking about it and babying it, hoping it would get better, but it only got worse? Or, have you had the opposite experience where you had a headache, and you were so busy that you paid zero attention to it, and then quickly it just went away? Our mind has a funny way of making things bigger when we focus on them, and smaller when we give them little attention.

When you are thinking about quitting, your mind comes up with lots of reasons to encourage you to quit, all because that is what you are focusing on. If you think about reasons to finish, your mind will come up with plenty of resources and reasons to help you finish, because that is how it works. Your mind pays you back whenever you pay attention to it.

In most sports, there is a visible finish line or an end goal. You can see your opponents, and there is a referee. In life, the finish line or end goal is invisible. You cannot always see it, which can make it easy to quit. Also, you do not always see your opponents, and the referee is your intuition or self-awareness. You could be moments away from winning, but because you cannot see the finish line or an opponent suddenly shows up out of nowhere, you give up too soon. Most of life has an invisible finish line because for most situations winning is a feeling more than an outcome.

In track and field, there will always be a line you need to push yourself toward. If you can sprint a 100-meter dash, but are unable to run the 200, push yourself an extra 10 meters of sprinting on the 100 until you train your body to handle it. That same theory can be seen in your mind as well. If you want to train yourself to win and never quit, set up intermittent milestones that you can push towards so that you are always challenging yourself but not burning yourself out. Keep training your mind to be positive by celebrating your victories. Look past all the noise and crap from other people and stay focused on your outcome. Look past the obstacles and push through the pain. When you get close to achieving your goal, set your sights just past the finish and push through, using all your pain as motivation. When you reach that point of victory, pause, look back and celebrate. Pain is temporary. The feeling of victory lasts a lifetime.

DON'T HELP THE BUTTERFLY

There is a story of a young boy beaming with excitement while holding the cocoon of a caterpillar in his hand. To his amazement, the cocoon was opening, and the soon to blossom butterfly was beginning to be born. As the boy watched the butterfly press its wings against the cocoon trying to get out, the boy thought it was stuck and wanted to help it. He picked up a very small pair of scissors and cut the cocoon open hoping the butterfly would quickly become freed. To his dismay, the butterfly fell to the ground and died. The boy soon learned that a butterfly needs the struggle of pressing against the cocoon to strengthen its wings. When he cut the cocoon, the butterfly got out before it was ready and did not yet have the strength to fly.

Just as the butterfly needs to struggle to gain its strength, we too need to understand that there are no shortcuts in life. Too many people get lost in their struggles and never understand that they are strengthening their wings. It is okay to help people in need, but do not help them so much that they learn to depend on you instead of growing their wings.

Life is tricky. On the path toward your dreams you may see what appears to be easy solutions and shortcuts, but do not be fooled by appearances. If something looks like an easy way out or too good to be true, pause and take the time to explore whether or not it is true, then make a decision.

Life has a fast lane and a slow lane, and there is also a back road. The back road is shorter. You may think it is faster, but beware because if you take it, you will be cheating. Even though it is tempting, it is not part of the path, and it will lead you astray. No matter how much you find yourself being tempted, do not cheat life. When you cheat, you are not only cheating yourself out of valuable life lessons, you are claiming a victory that you did not earn. When you claim something that you did not earn, life will take it away from you.

Learn from the butterfly. Accept your struggles as life lessons. Do not get lost in pain, but dig around for what you can learn and then grow your wings so that you can prosper and fulfill your dreams.

BE GRATEFUL

If you were to ignore or forget everything that I have written, remember only one thing. Gratitude solves all problems. Be grateful for what you have and be grateful for what you have lost. Be grateful for what lies ahead and what you have left behind. Be grateful for your pain because it can become your guide. Be grateful for your blessings and for the opportunity to bless others.

Gratitude is like the eye of a tornado. The more focused you are on what you are grateful for, the faster you will draw more goodness into your life. Gratitude is a feeling backed by words. Speak and feel gratitude and your life will quickly change.

Epilogue

"Be happy for this moment.
This moment is your life."
— Omar Khayyam

When I first committed to being one of the authors of this book, it was because I realized that there are other guys and gals who are in the same situation I was in. If someone is not doing well in school, or dropped out like me, it does not mean they have to brand themselves as a failure for the rest of their life.

Just because someone is trained to think that they can only succeed in life and be happy by staying in a comfort zone and conforming to the cookie-cutter reality, it does not mean that they have to believe that lie. Everyone has their unique way of thinking and learning. There are a lot of people like me who do not want to fit into a pre-determined reality. Instead, they want to chart their own course in life and live on their terms.

Since our mission in *Think Gen Why* is to inspire our generation and anyone else who wants to help make our world a better place, I saw this book as an opportunity to turn my story into a resource for others to gain the courage and tools to take responsibility for their life.

Before writing this book, never before had anyone challenged me to think about what I believe and to put it in writing in a way that could help guide my life and the lives of others. Working with our writing coach and mentor, David Strauss, helped me to identify the key lessons that I wrote about. Coming from a background of being a high school dropout, believing that I could do this was a big shift in my thinking and self-image.

The fact that this book is now published proves the five points that I wrote about.
- If you have the courage to be yourself, anything is possible.
- When you change your mindset, you really do change your entire life.
- When you raise your people standards, you begin to look at life differently.
- Becoming the leader of your own life changes everything.
- If you develop a winning philosophy, there are no limits to what you can accomplish.

It is my hope that the lessons I shared will inspire others to forgive themselves for their failures and begin to see that their past does not determine their future. You alone are responsible for the rest of your life.

If your life is perfectly imperfect, then you are ready to take your life to the next level. No matter what you are doing, get out there and go to work on yourself. Get out there, stop surviving, and start to thrive. Take that leap of faith. Believe in yourself and go after your dreams. If you fail, get your ass back up and go at it again. It is your life. Never quit believing in yourself or your potential.

If you ever start feeling low and dis-empowered, try something different that will challenge you and make you feel vibrant and alive. Do not mope around and get lost in negative thinking. Find a way to reconnect with your happiness. Go for a walk. Go for a hike. Go to a pet store and pet the puppies and kittens. Drive your car around the city or in the mountains. Get up and do something different so that you can achieve the happiness and fulfillment you have been searching for.

Any issue you have can be fixed over time. Whether you are at the top of your world or trying to figure out who you are and what you want, if you apply the insights shared in my five lessons, your life can only change for the better.

I challenge you to be the leader of your life. Do not wait for happiness. Do not delay building your self-confidence. Create and test a new theory for your life. Raise your standards and be willing to fail your way to success.

Do not assume that your life will go on forever. Face your problems and find solutions. Stop running from your past and from your fears, and begin sprinting toward your future. When you stop running from your past, it is still behind you, so you might as well look forward. You cannot change what happened to you. You can only change what it means to you, and you can choose the direction of your life.

Allow your mind to do what it does best. Think.

Acknowledgements

Writing this book could not be done without our awesome coach, David Strauss. He helped us organize our thoughts and gave our group amazing ideas, and more importantly, he gave us his time.

I could not have done this without any of my brothers, Kyler, Matt, Ryan, Eric, and Ethan, or without the support of my family.

I appreciate all the great teachers I had throughout elementary school, middle school, and high school. Although I did not make it to the finish, I saw efforts until the end.

Special thanks to all my close friends and all the people God has blessed into my life. Thank you to my brothers from school, Noah H., Nic M., Connor B., Caleb W., and my best friend that I met through cheer, Anthony F.

Shout out to all my cheer friends and old school friends! Without all of you, none of this would have been possible. Thank you for always believing in me.

I would also like to thank my sisters, Katie, Emily, and Amanda. I love you all very much.

Mom & Dad, I cannot even begin to describe how much I appreciate all you have done for me. Thank you for always believing in me. Most importantly, thank you for setting such a great example and teaching me how to think, not what to think. I love you!

BOOK THREE

YOU ARE THE WALL

FIVE LESSONS FOR TURNING OBSTACLES INTO OPPORTUNITIES

• MATTHEW WOOD •

Prologue

*"It is when you lose sight of yourself, that you lose your way.
To keep your truth in sight you must keep yourself in sight,
and the world to you should be a mirror to reflect you—your image;
the world should be a mirror that you reflect upon."*
— C. JoyBell C.

Who am I? Why am I here? What is my purpose? These are questions that everyone asks themselves at some point in their life, especially young adults. I know that I have asked these questions of myself many times as far back as I can remember. The many possible answers would circle my brain for hours in the hopes of finding the true meaning of my life.

While growing up, all I wanted was someone to help me understand my purpose and point me in the right direction so that I could figure out who I am and what I want. Looking back now that I am 23 years young, if I had known that there was a shortcut to the answers, I can only imagine how different my childhood would have been. I discovered the shortcut when someone told me that I could not make sense of my life or make any changes in my life until I changed my story. It was not until after I screwed up many times as a teenager that I began to understand who I am and why I am here, and what it meant to change my story.

Everyone has their own story about who they are and what happened to them. The story is the sum-total of all their beliefs based on the meaning they have given to their experiences. It is what makes someone who they are. For some people, their story is one of continuous struggle, failed expectations, and being a victim of life's circumstances. For others, their story is one of gaining strength and courage through overcoming challenges. They see themselves as the hero of their own life. We are the authors of our story because we get to choose the beliefs and emotions we assign to our life experiences. We change our story by changing the meaning we have given to the events of our life.

My life story has been a long winding road that eventually led to a fifteen-foot brick wall that stood in the way of me furthering my life. When I first came upon this wall, I did not know what to do. I was living my life the way I was taught to live it, but no one ever told me about this wall, and so when I came upon it, I had no idea what to do. Every time I would try and go over or around it, the wall would just get taller and wider. It was as if the wall adapted to my thoughts and feelings. With complete frustration, I eventually stopped trying to get over or around the wall. Instead, I sat in front of it and stared at it with the hopes of understanding where it came from.

I stared at the wall for so long that I could not tell the difference between me and the wall. And then one day, I figured it out: I was the wall. Each brick represented one of my fears. I had accumulated enough fears over time that they slowly and subtly stacked high and wide enough to become a wall. I had become a prisoner of my fears.

My wall was not built overnight. In fact, I did not even know I was building a wall. When I was young, no one taught me that it is up us to face our fears and overcome them, or fall victim to them. If we avoid facing our fears, they do not go away. They just incubate and eventually grow into something that can become a barricade between us and our dreams, and eventually shut down our entire life.

As I sat in front of the wall, soaking in the realization that I had created my wall based on my thoughts and beliefs, it occurred to me that my wall was there to show me where I was weak, and where I needed to grow the most. It was not an obstacle, but a place for me to rest and pause so that I could reflect upon my experiences and learn from them. This led me to uncover five lessons which now form the foundation of how I live my life.

1) Change your story, change your life.
2) Forgiveness is the ultimate solvent
3) Identify your "Why"
4) Turn your bricks into bridges
5) Live with gratitude

These same five lessons can help anyone who wants to improve their life.

LESSON ONE

CHANGE YOUR STORY, CHANGE YOUR LIFE

"In every change, in every falling leaf, there is some pain, some beauty. And that's the way new leaves grow."
— Amit Ray

Your story is the backbone of who you are and how you live your life. It is a collection of habits and decisions based on what you believe and how you see life. From the moment you wake up to the moment you go to sleep, you are living your story.

My life and my story started out great. I had almost anything any young boy would want. I had a solid family with parents who truly loved me and cared about me. They provided for all my needs—lots of food, a safe home, plenty of love, toys galore, and an amazing Christmas every year. But, as I grew older I began to understand life and its challenges, and my storybook life began to collapse.

When I was 12 years old, my parents got divorced. My mom walked out on our family; it seemed like she was leaving us behind forever. This left a hole inside me, and I began to fear commitment to anything I ever tried to do. I could not commit to a single task because I had the fear that it would burn me at some point in time. This fear became the foundation of my wall. I also started fearing abandonment, loss of love, and rejection.

A few years down the road, at age 16, I was in some trouble with the law and got arrested. This year-long experience added three more bricks to my wall—failure, embarrassment, and shame. Not even a few months after I was arrested, my dad had heart surgery. The health complications weren't overly serious, but I was afraid of losing my father, and I also did not want to become unhealthy like him. This was the first time I ever felt the fear of ill health. It was also the first time I realized the true power and potential of fear. It is okay to be afraid of something, but it is not good to let it stop you from moving forward. I let this fear of ill-health empower me to make positive changes in my life instead of keeping me stuck in front of my wall. Fear became my fuel because my hunger for change outweighed the anchor of my fear. I knew that health and wellness would forever become a part of my life.

I barely made it through high school, and at age 19, I left for college. As college went on, my life felt like a train going downhill with no brakes. My grades sucked, I could not stay focused, I was lonely and unsure of myself. My wall of fears came to a head. Drug use and partying were consuming me from the inside out. One evening, while partying with some friends, things got out of hand to the point where for the first time in my life, I got down on my knees and prayed because I was afraid for a friend's life. By some miracle, my friend did not die. After years of dancing with my fears and making reckless choices, this event was the trigger for me to face my fears. I got angry with my life, tapped into some courage, demolished my wall, and started taking responsibility for my own life.

I was going to college to become a professional baseball player. Even though I was on a baseball scholarship and was fortunate enough to play at the Division-II level, some things are just not meant to be. One week before my 22nd birthday I dropped out of college, said my goodbyes to the baseball team, packed up, and moved back home to Colorado to help my family financially. How was I supposed to live the college life when my dad was facing eviction?

Thinking that dropping out of college was rock bottom, it quickly got worse. Two weeks after being home, my dad went in for a four-way bypass surgery. Talk about rock bottom, in a matter of weeks, I went from being a college kid getting his life together to running the family business. Trying to save our house and lives, I busted my ass for months, successfully digging us out of this hole.

The weight on my shoulders was quite heavy, and I could easily have felt like a victim of circumstances and become resentful for having dropped out of college and giving up my baseball scholarship and my dream to become a professional baseball player. Instead, I realized that I had a choice about what all this meant to me and that I could choose the ending to this chapter in the story of my life. This is when I truly understood that you could not change your life until you change your story. I decided that since I cannot change the events of my past, I accepted them as the dues that I had to pay to begin my journey of becoming a man.

Even though I am now only 23 years young, I have experienced many different challenges and battles that have shaped me into who I am today. The courage, strength, and faith that I have gained have helped to prepare me for anything. It all comes down to understanding that we decide how to respond to life's battles and we choose the ending to each chapter of our story.

Through the insight I have gained from experience, I have identified seven simple steps that anyone can use to reconstruct their story and create a new one that empowers their future. Think of these steps as a way to transform the bricks built from your fears into bricks that form the foundation of the bridge toward your dreams.

1) Create your storyboard
2) Identify your anchor life events
3) List the leaks
4) Link the lessons
5) Rewrite your story
6) Establish a new pattern
7) Celebrate

Everyone has a story, and every story has walls. We unknowingly build our walls beginning early in life, and we will continue to do so until something happens to jolt us and make us aware of the story we are living that is creating our walls.

Your wall is not there to stop you, but to guide you. It is a teacher because it represents the negativity that you allowed to affect you, which is the very thing you need to overcome to advance your life. Your wall is mental and emotional feedback. It shows you what you have been thinking about most of the time and the main emotions that rule your life.

Understanding your wall relates back to your story, but it is only the negative or disruptive events in your life that add bricks to your wall. Anything you can think of that made you sad, angry, embarrassed or uncomfortable contributed to your wall. Some of the bricks could be specific days where something horrific happened, and your life completely changed. But they could also be the way your parents talked to you over the years, or a school bully you forgot existed. Anger problems can relate back to your father yelling at you as a kid. It is both the small and big things, often repeated many times, that can damage you more than you realize, because they eat away at your self-esteem and cause you to question your abilities. Figuring these things out can be unsettling, but it is also the beginning of change.

Deep thought is necessary for you to look back upon your life and recall as many of the challenges as you can that formed your wall. It is not easy to remember all the disruptive events or negative influences from your early years, but since they form the foundation of your wall, it is worth the effort. The real work is in understanding and identifying the brick that was created as a result of each negative event. When I say "understand," I mean to get to the core of what happened and the influence it had on your life.

Digging deep into my past was not easy for me. I had to have a conversation with someone about my past, and they helped to pull it out of me—to identify my negative emotions that turned into bricks. When we did this, I broke down emotionally because it was such a major reality check for me. It was okay to break down because it meant that I got to the core of my pain. It was a big step for me to understand my childhood and to begin breaking the foundation of my wall so that I could change my story.

Changing your story takes courage. For most people, it is much easier to skate through life and not face the uncertainty of revisiting their past. For me and others who have faced insurmountable challenges, it was a must. If someone were to ask me what they need to do to change their story, I would give them the following seven steps which create the framework for making changes to your life.

Create Your Storyboard

Retrace your life events from as far back as you can remember. Identify every significant event that has ever happened in your life that you remember and that had an emotional impact on you. Think of the good, the bad, and the ugly. Think of everything that has shaped you into the person you are today—how you act, how you speak, how you think, how you feel about life, and how you make decisions. Write these down in a list from earliest memory forward.

IDENTIFY YOUR ANCHOR LIFE EVENTS

From the list above, separate out the life-changing events, both positive and disruptive, that completely interrupted your life and altered your emotions, dreams, or current way of living. Examples of positive events would be graduation, marriage, a new career, or accomplishment of a major goal. Examples of disruptive events would be the loss of a loved one, an accident, injury, illness or disease, an unexpected career change, or the end of a relationship. As you recall these events, write them down in numerical order, starting with your earliest memory.

List the Leaks

Events in one part of your life can leak into and affect other areas of your life without you even knowing it. Identify the specific disruptive anchor events that leaked into other parts of your life. For example, a fear of loss of love may prevent you from allowing a romantic relationship into your life. But, it may also prevent you from welcoming close friends into your life.

Link the Lessons

Your past does affect your future. The meaning you give to your experiences determines how you make decisions in the future. Identify the meaning and lesson you assigned to each of your anchor life events.

Rewrite Your Story

Once you begin to see how certain events impacted your life, you can begin to change those things about yourself. Cutting one chain link can cure other issues that were connected. For each anchor life event that you assigned a negative or painful meaning, forgive that person or event and identify a new and empowering meaning. For example, if you escaped a painful relationship, you now have more clarity about what you do not want and what you do want in your next relationship.

Establish Your New Pattern

Ask yourself game-changing questions:
- What is my new identity?
- How will I act differently now that I have re-written my past?
- Where can I find a mentor and a coach?
- What type of people do I want to surround myself with?
- What negative people do I need to purge from my life?
- What new actions do I need to take right now to begin my new pattern?

CELEBRATE

Do something right away to celebrate your new story. Buy yourself a gift or do something that will anchor your new identity. Do something significant and monumental so that it feels like a real celebration, something that makes you feel proud of yourself.

LESSON TWO

FORGIVENESS...
THE ULTIMATE SOLVENT

*"When you forgive, you in no way change the past,
but you sure do change the future."*
— Bernard Meltzer

If fear and pain create the bricks to your wall, then forgiveness is the ultimate solvent that helps to crumble your wall so you can change your story. For me, forgiveness means forgiving yourself and others. It is when you let go of the pain and blame caused by harm, and you no longer allow it to affect you emotionally. When I look back on my life, a lot of my bricks were from lack of forgiveness. I was holding onto the past instead of looking toward my future.

Although I do not remember a lot of my childhood, I do remember how I would always react to anything and everything. It did not matter if it was big or small—I always found a way to react angrily. I would fight with my family because I did not agree with their opinion. I reacted to my classmates based on things they would say about me, and to people who belittled me about my goals and dreams. I endlessly wasted my energy on others who enjoyed seeing me upset. I carried this hurt around for a long time, and it was definitely at least one of the bricks in my wall, if not more.

Even though I did not know it at the time, every time I reacted to someone, I was making my wall bigger and stronger. The reality is, we live in a world with lots of different types of people, and everyone thinks their own way. I wanted everyone to think my way, and when they did not, I would react instead of trying to see their point of view.

I now understand that not everything in life requires a reaction. You do not have to voice your opinion every time someone says or does something that you do not like or agree with. Sometimes you just have to let things go and not take them personally. People are going to think what they think, and at the end of the day, it only affects you if you let it.

When I stopped living in the past and started to care less about what others thought about me, and more about what I thought about myself, it allowed me to find more happiness in life. I was able to do this when I realized that whenever we forgive someone or ourselves, the act of forgiveness is like a solvent that unglues the bricks from each other.

No matter where you are in your story right now, the past is still the past, and you can't change it. You can carry it around like a wet blanket, or you can forgive yourself and others. I was my own worst critic, and I still am. We all are. We can be so hard on ourselves sometimes. Take a step back and realize we are only human. Humans make mistakes. Forgive others and yourself, and your wall will begin to break down.

LESSON THREE

Identify Your "Why"

*"Choose your friends with caution;
plan your future with purpose, and frame your life with faith."*
— *Thomas S. Monson*

When you combine the seven steps for changing your story with the power of forgiveness, you are on track for big changes in your life. The glue that pulls all this together is your "why." This is your action motivator. It is the mental and emotional fire that gets you up early and keeps you up late.

For most people, they find their *why* when they hit rock bottom. But for other people, it comes when they reach a point of extreme dissatisfaction with their life, and they demand change. Either way, your *why* is the trigger for a massive change that you are hungry for and are committed to taking action towards—immediately and consistently, regardless of the obstacles that may push against you.

I found my *why* when I hit rock bottom. I consider it to be a major part of my story and is the reason I was able to bust down my wall. My *why* is taking care of my family and focusing on my dreams. Those are the only two things I need to get me going each day.

My family is everything to me. They are the only ones that have truly been there for me when I hit rock bottom. Yes, they can be difficult to deal with at times, but all that matters is that we love and accept each other for who we are. At the end of the day, I am grateful that I can help them if they ever need it—whether it is financial, physical, emotional, or spiritual.

When I was busting down my wall, I realized that if I do not take care of myself, I cannot take care of my family. In order to be caring and generous toward my family, and others, I also have to be very selfish and focus on my happiness and success. It is all too easy for me to be a very giving person and spread my energy to anyone who reaches out for it and then forgets about my own needs. I believe that true happiness comes from filling your cup first. How can you help others when you cannot even help yourself? I work very hard at everything I put my mind to, and deserve to be rewarded for my success. I fill my cup first, and then my family's when they need it. This is how I stay motivated.

***

It was a rough journey up until the time I discovered my *why*. If someone were to ask me how they could discover their *why* without going through a life crisis or reaching a point of utter dissatisfaction with their life, I would suggest asking themselves seven simple questions to help them figure out what they want to do.

1) What wrong do you want to make right in your life?
2) What makes you feel alive, motivated, and vibrant?
3) What type of impact do you want to have on others?
4) What are your greatest strengths?
5) What are you willing to let go of to make it happen?
6) What would stop you from following through?
7) What do you have to lose and gain?

Everyone's *why* is going to be different. To answer these questions, you have to set aside some "me time." Find a place where you can shut off your cell phone and disconnect from all distractions. This will give you the mental space to think and listen to your heart and mind.

I recommend sitting down and writing out the answers to these questions. This is a powerful exercise because it gets you thinking about your purpose here on Earth. When you think about your *why,* you want to get real personal with yourself. No one else is going to read this unless you share it with them, so be brutally honest with your answers.

There is a saying that I have heard many times that may help you think about the direction of your life.

> "Success isn't judged by how much money is in your bank account, how many cars you have, or how big your house is, but by how many people show up to your funeral."

Once you find your *why,* it is not like your life is suddenly going to change, and everything is going to go smoothly. In reality, things can still be rough for a while because you are going against years of patterns and habits. There is always the residue of the past that will show up as obstacles and distractions. It is up to you to press forward and stay consistent.

We all run into obstacles daily. They are a part of life. The question is, how do you handle them? Do you tuck your tail between your legs and let them overpower you? Or, do you push back against the obstacles and stay focused on your new path? If your *why* is strong enough and you have a truly burning desire that motivates you from within, pushing back with your fiery desire is the easiest way to move through your obstacles.

Discovering your purpose and having a *why* is not just a good idea. It is a basic principle in the formula for achievement. A life purpose comes in different shapes and sizes. A pastor's *why* is to spread the gospel.

A mother's *why* is to love and care for her children properly. An artist's *why* is to express their creativity. When you discover your purpose, it will not feel like something that you have to do, but that you want to do.

I have my life's purpose written down. Every time I recite my *why* to myself, it gets me all fired up because I believe in it so strongly. Sometimes I get tears in my eyes because I see how far I have come since hitting rock bottom.

Once you discover your life purpose, you can move forward boldly with faith and courage.

LESSON FOUR

TURN YOUR BRICKS INTO BRIDGES

"True teachers use themselves as bridges over which they invite their students to cross; then, having facilitated their crossing, joyfully collapse, encouraging them to create bridges of their own."
— Nikos Kazantzakis

When I busted down my wall, I started taking the same bricks that blocked my path and started using them to build bridges to my dreams. I took the bricks of anger and blame and used them for forgiveness. I took fear and turned it into courage, turned stubbornness into being teachable, and turned rejection into self-love.

Building bridges did so many wonderful things for my life. My happiness increased, my motivation ignited, I met amazing people, and I came upon unexpected opportunities.

My biggest bridge is love. I believe we all deserve to experience love and to be loved. The love I speak of is the love of life, people, friends, pets, things, places—really anything that we find ourselves interested in or drawn to. You must allow yourself to be loved as well. These two go hand-in-hand—loving and being loved. This also allows for all kinds of people to flow into your life for all the right reasons.

My second bridge is courage. I value courage so highly because I lacked it when I was a kid. I used to feel lesser than everyone else and always sought out the approval of others. The more I developed courage, the easier it was for me to pursue my dreams. Believing in yourself—having the courage to step out of your comfort zone and take risks is fundamental to turning your bricks into bridges.

My third bridge is being teachable. One of the things that always got me in trouble was my need to be right all the time. When I hit rock bottom, I finally realized that it was *my* ideas and *my* thinking that got me in trouble. If I wanted to improve my life, I had to improve my thinking. That is when I discovered the importance of having a coach and a mentor and having a high willingness to learn. A mentor has the results you want and can teach you from experience. But they can only teach someone who is willing to listen and learn, and willing to ditch unproductive patterns, habits, and beliefs. A coach helps you create strategies and action plans and helps you to keep your thoughts, ideas, and behaviors consistent with your ambitions. Mentors and coaches are like bridges over troubled waters. If you walk across the bridge and pay attention to the signs, you can avoid drowning. I attribute all my progress to having found the right mentors and coaches.

Everyone's bridges are different. When you rewrite your story, you get to decide the new meaning of each brick, and you also get to design the exact bridge to the life you want to live. It all whittles down to one simple idea: we are all looking for happiness.

We all find our happiness in different places. Even though happiness is a state of mind, and not a destination, knowing what you enjoy most, what makes you most happy, is where you should focus the building of your bridges.

If you follow the seven steps to changing your story, forgive yourself and others, and answer the seven questions to finding your *why*, you will find it easy to change the meaning of your bricks and build the bridge to your dreams.

Follow these three steps to help you turn your bricks into bridges.
1) Identify the bricks that represent your greatest pain.
2) If you were to forgive the people and situations that those bricks represent, what new meaning could you give to each of those bricks?
3) What would you be willing to create in your life with your newly defined bricks?

Knowing that my most important bridge is love, here's a challenge that will help you become clear about yours. Do this before or after you answer the above three questions. I call it the *24-Hour Love Challenge*. Doing this is how I fell back in love with my life.

I challenge you to go a full day spreading as much love as you can by doing simple, thoughtful things that make people feel loved and significant. Give flowers to someone you care about. Call an old friend and express your gratitude for their friendship. Give money to a homeless person. Visit the cancer ward of a children's hospital. Give money to someone anonymously. Talk to a homeless person and listen to their story without judgment or interrupting. Give thanks to the store clerk, by name. It's amazing how far a simple "thank you" goes.

There are different types of love. Try to be your best in all of them. Be creative for one full day and see how you feel. People love to be around someone who is uplifting and cares. Do all this without expecting anything in return.

Never stop loving.

LESSON FIVE
LIVE WITH GRATITUDE

"Gratitude makes sense of our past, brings peace for today, and creates a vision for tomorrow."
— *Melody Beattie*

As crazy at it may sound, I am very grateful that the first part of my life was so messed up, because I learned some valuable lessons that are going to make a big difference in the rest of my life. Every life lesson has its value. At the top of the list is the importance of being grateful.

What does it mean to be grateful? For me, it means being thankful for all the blessings in my life—both big and small. More than that, gratitude is also a skill. Anyone can say *thank you,* but true gratitude is when you realize how fortunate you are to have what you have in your life. The skill is when you know how to recognize those blessings, and you do not take them for granted. Some people are raised to be grateful while others can learn it over time if they have the right people in their life to show them.

Here in the United States, we are very lucky because the vast majority of people have been given access to simple luxuries along with tremendous opportunities to improve their life. Those basic luxuries include safe drinking water, plenty of food, and the very clothes on your back. There are countless opportunities to chase your dreams and turn them into a reality. We need to be grateful for these. The fact that you are literate enough to read this book makes you luckier than most people in our world. Some people in this world will live their whole life only dreaming of having the very basic luxuries that we enjoy and take for granted. Even though our system is not perfect, if you connect to the right people and situations, you can find yourself with plenty to be grateful for. Never forget that.

My belief in the importance of gratitude has roots in my Christian beliefs. I start and end my day with feelings of gratitude because I have learned how much it improves my life and allows me to bless others. Every morning when I wake up, and every night before bed I give thanks to God for my family, friends, food, clothing, a roof over my head, and the ability to make decisions. I give thanks for life itself and all it has to offer. These are what I am blessed with, and I never take them for granted.

For a lot of people, gratitude is an on/off switch in the background of their life. When things are going well, they forget to be grateful. When life starts to fall apart, and they hope and pray for a miracle, they give thanks when the miracle shows up. For me, gratitude is a lifestyle. I believe that we need to be grateful at all times in our life, especially when things are tough. The more consistently you live with gratitude, the more blessings God brings into your life. I do not go a single day without telling God I am thankful to be alive. Even if you do not believe in God, whatever you believe in, love it daily, and unconditionally. If you live a grateful life, you will see *miracles* show up every day.

There is an old wives' tale that says, *"do not sweat the small stuff,"* which means do not worry about things that aren't important. This saying has been pounded into my head since I was a kid. I see it differently. When it comes to gratitude, I think everything is important, even the small stuff. I am a fan of the small things in life. The small things are the hidden joys in life. They are the daily activities that make life, life.

Most importantly, an attitude of gratitude also translates to being respectful and having good manners. A simple thank you can save a life. You can only know your own problems; not what others are facing. We all have our battles. In a world full of violence and hate, let's all try to spread some good. We should always go the extra mile for others. When you treat people the way you want to be treated, you pave the road to happiness.

Never go a day without sharing your gratitude. You never know whose life you will impact or when the things you love will be taken from you. I smile every time someone thanks me for holding the door or saying, "bless you." It is in the little wins in life that I find enjoyment.

Being a grateful person relates back to spreading love—which is my biggest bridge in life. Some of your hardest days might be the greatest days of the lives of people who are less fortunate than you, so live with gratitude! Spread love and do the little things. Have fun with it. Love life!

Epilogue

I am just a 23 year-old guy that got lucky enough to make some mistakes early in life and then found some people to help me correct my path. I do not have it all figured out, but I do know that the things I went through have shaped me into the man I am today, and can also help you mold your life into the reality of your dreams.

I have been through some shit in life, and I know that I am not alone. There are a lot of guys and gals my age who are facing challenges and need help. If your life is pushing against you right now, remember that you do not have to stare at your wall forever. There are people who can help you, but you have to want to help yourself first. Other people have turned their walls into bridges, and you can, too.

I encourage you to get on a real level with yourself and find out what you truly believe in. If you have a hard time doing this, reach out to someone for help. We are all on our own journeys, but you do not have to be alone. Find a mentor. Find a coach. Tap into a network of people who will support your ambitions.

The greatest piece of advice that one of my mentors gave me was to just "ask." If you want to do something and you are not sure how to do it, then find someone who already has what you want, and ask them for help. Asking someone for help can make a miracle show up in your life faster than if you tried to figure it out on your own.

I challenge you to take control of your life. If you are ready for your life to change, then figure out what your story is and what you need to do to change it. Identify who and what you need to forgive, and do it. Identify your *why* and focus on gratitude. Write down what you want in life, find the people who can help you get there, and put the action plans to the test.

I know I make it sound easy, but it is not. The best things in life do not come easy, because overcoming the struggle is what gives you strength. The battle is always between your fears and your dreams. If you have the courage to persevere and you surround yourself with the right people, your dreams will win. Stick with it and see the results pour in.

Enjoyed this book?
Share the love...
Tweet, post, Insta...
#ThinkGenWhy
Facebook.com/ThinkGenWhy

Review on Amazon. Go to:
www.ThinkGenWhyBook.com

Acknowledgements

To all of you, I give thanks...

Special thanks to my father, Jeff Wood, for supporting me through my journey of life. He always sacrificed himself for his kids, and for that, I am forever thankful.

To my mom and two sisters, thank you for always being there for me. To my friends...those in my life daily and the ones I haven't talked to in years, every single one of you had an impact on my life, and I thank you.

To my mastermind...the network of achievers and go-getters who brought a newly found energy into my life, your high vibration of love and courage put me into a different world. I know I can ask anything of you, and that's an amazing relationship to have.

To my mentor, Tony Grebmeier, you reached out to me through the kindness of your heart. I have never met a more giving person in my life, so thank you.

To anyone who ever doubted me or told me I was not good enough. You are the reason my competitive spirit runs wild, and I will prove you wrong.

And lastly, thanks to our writing coach and mentor, David Strauss. You are an exceptional human being. Thank you for guiding us through the journey of writing this book so that we can make a difference in this world together.

Most importantly, I want to thank God. I believe that he saved me, even when I was not a believer. If that is not love, then I do not know what is.

Thank you,

Matthew Wood

BOOK FOUR

SLACKLINER'S MINDSET

SEVEN KEYS TO BALANCE WHEN LIFE GIVES YOU WOBBLES

• RYAN MILLER •

Prologue

"It is not by muscle, speed, or physical dexterity that great things are achieved, but by reflection, force of character, and judgment."
— Marcus Tullius Cicero

When was the last time you sat down alone to have a conversation about your own life with yourself?

For many people, their lives are continuously cluttered with responsibilities and habitual thought patterns that they never really take a moment to put everything aside, become totally present, and give conscious thought to important questions that can shape the quality of their lives. These days, our world is so full of distractions that the majority of people are not spending enough time alone figuring themselves out. This alone time is important because it allows for powerful self-reflection and can be a catalyst for growth and change.

Far too many people are too concerned about fitting in and being accepted by others instead of discovering who they are or even what they truly want in life. I know because I was that person, and you may be, too. But that all changes with this book and the life lessons I learned that I am now sharing.

Even though I am just an average kid, I was lucky enough to be introduced to some really smart people at a young age, and what they taught me has been a game changer for my entire life. I want to take what I have learned and add value to other guys and gals in my generation by showing them a different way of doing things.

I want people to know that they can overcome self-limiting beliefs. They do not have to fit in or be a genius or do things that do not align with their passion. It is okay to think differently. They do not have to drift through college or life. There is a way to find your purpose and your passion, and as you read the pages that follow, I will show you how.

It comes down to this. Most people struggle with confidence and self-esteem or do not have a true sense of purpose or passion because they are not asking themselves the right questions about who they are and what they want out of life. People habitually ask themselves negative questions like:

- What's wrong with me?
- How come nothing works for me?
- Why can't I figure this out?

You cannot ask a negative question and get a positive answer. Your questions determine your focus. Better questions to ask yourself would be:

- Who am I?
- What do I really want?
- Am I truly happy?
- Is what I am doing contributing toward my desires?
- Who or what do I need to let go of to improve my life?
- Have I learned anything new recently?
- What can I do better and how can I be better?

If you were to ask yourself these questions right now and answer them with full honesty, would you say your life is balanced and in control, or is it wobbly and out of control? Do you feel like life is happening to you, or are you confidently in charge of the direction of your life? Are you happy with your level of health and fitness? Do you have a lifestyle that you enjoy? When you look in the mirror, are you proud of your body or ashamed of how you look?

Imagine how different your life would be if you asked yourself these types of questions on a regular basis and you took corrective action when things were not the way you wanted them to be. Looking at my own life, when I started asking myself these questions, it ultimately connected me with my sense of purpose and gave me a clear direction for my life.

Intro to the Slackliner's Mindset

*"Do not dwell on the past, do not dream of the future.
Concentrate the mind on the present moment."*
— Buddha

My name is Ryan Miller. I am 20 years old and attend Colorado State University to get my Bachelor of Science degree in health and exercise. When I walk around my college campus, I see so many students who look like they are stranded or lost. Many are going to school just because that is what the norm is and what they think they should be doing, but they do not have any real direction or life purpose. I have met plenty of kids with great ideas and *some* ambition to try something different, yet there is this underlying pain that they do not believe that they can achieve the success they truly want. They end up taking the "safe route" and go for a job they know they can get, which does not always line up with their interest or passion.

No matter what the reason for this gap—whether it be from not knowing how, too much work, or limiting beliefs, I knew that I did not want to be a person who is lost or without focus. I wanted to have a clear direction for my life, and I found it.

Fitness and health have always been a big interest and priority of mine. The future I saw for myself just a couple of years ago was getting a degree, becoming a personal trainer, and then working for 10 to 15 years until I had put enough money together to open my own gym. I was driven by wanting to make a lot of money and having the freedom to do as I please. I knew that owning a business was my best option for creating something for myself that would allow me to achieve the income needed for my desired lifestyle. It was not until I was 20 that I realized I could follow my passion of health and fitness, and create something bigger than I had originally imagined—something that would allow me to impact and change the lives of thousands, and in turn pay me more than I ever thought possible by just being your basic personal trainer.

Just like the rest of the world, I am probably not a whole lot different from you. Our personal life experiences have shaped us into who we are and who we are to become, yet at our core, we are very much the same. We eat, breathe, communicate, connect, love, dream, and desire to be better and experience more of what life has to offer. We each have our victories and our setbacks and plenty of challenges to overcome.

I was raised with many of the same challenges that others faced in their childhood. I grew up with a single parent my entire life. My mom has been working her ass off ever since I was born to provide the best she can for my sister and me. As hard as she worked, I always felt some stress from financial pressure on our family, and so I would usually not ask for gifts because I did not want to be a burden. A big part of my reasoning was because my Mom had lost her job during the 2008 recession and was unemployed for a year and a half. It is crazy how much a lifestyle can change when financial pressure hits.

Despite all her struggles, my mother is a smart, strong, and resourceful lady. When things were scarce, I watched her push through the hard times and find a way to get by. She became a savvy coupon saver and was like those people you see on TV, sometimes saving more than she spent. There were no handouts in our family. Her philosophy was if I wanted something, I would have to work and earn money to get it myself, and that is precisely what I did.

I came from a town where many kids were given allowances or handed money from their parents. I did not have that. Momma Miller instilled in me a go-getter attitude and strong work ethic. She pushed me to hustle and taught me that if I wanted money, I needed to work for it. I started saving money as early as the sixth grade to achieve my goal of buying my first car. I was always doing odd jobs like working on yards, shoveling driveways, handyman stuff, selling pizza coupons door to door, and other creative endeavors. But your boy made it! At 16 I got my license and purchased my first car—a white 2000 Dodge Durango. Man, life was good—until I realized how much gas that baby burned up and that insurance was not cheap. I had to keep hustling and keep working. When I was working one of my jobs at the local Dairy Queen, I realized how shitty eight bucks an hour is. The work itself was not hard, but the fact that I was working so much just to pay for my car and food did not seem right. There had to be a better way.

I found the better way. A big shift in my life happened in 2013 during my junior year of high school. I became involved in a network marketing company. Whether you think network marketing is good or bad doesn't matter. What changed for me during that time was for once in my life I was surrounded by people who were internally driven, had dreams and aspirations, and actually cared and wanted me to succeed. People were optimistic about the future, talking about what could happen instead of why things could not happen. I met one of the top producers in the company, Tony Grebmeier, who became my mentor. At the time, I did not even know what a mentor was, but I quickly found out. He started teaching me about personal development and how to think like an entrepreneur, which was in sharp contrast to how I was being taught to think in school. He taught me one simple lesson that everyone should learn and live their life by:

> *"If you want to be successful in something, find someone who has already done what you want, and do what they did!"*

If you find someone who has what you want, and they are willing to teach and mentor you, you can get there a hell of a lot faster than trying to figure it out on your own or by following the advice of people who have failed.

Being in that network marketing environment also taught me how to use my imagination again and to dream big. Up until then, I felt like my imagination had been shut down to fit into the academic mindset. My other mentor, Michelle Barns, always used to say a "JOB" stands for *"Just Over Broke,"* because with most jobs you can only trade time for money. I was taught that it is better to make your money work for you.

Breaking away from the job mentality, tapping into the power of my imagination, and learning the importance of personal development, brought back lots of creative juices and gave me the confidence to pursue my real ambition of wanting to work in the health and fitness industry as a personal trainer and wellness coach.

As an avid athlete, I have always been someone who loves to try new things and to challenge myself. One of the most fun challenges I have taken on is learning how to slackline. A slackline is like a circus tightrope. You have to walk across a narrow, high-tension, seat-belt-like webbing tied between two trees—without falling. Even though many people see it as just a physical challenge, I see it as a mindset that can be applied to all of life.

The parallels between slacklining and learning how to do something new in life are perfect. When taking up slacklining for the first time it looks easy. But once you take the first step, you are in for a surprise. You are unbalanced, new to the experience, and not sure of the correct way to go about it. You stand up and then fall. You try again and fall. You fall so many times that it is easy to get frustrated and give up. But like anything new in life, there is a learning curve that you need to go through to get better and a mindset that you need to develop to stay balanced. The same strategy that it takes to walk across a slackline is what it takes to get real results in your life. It is the perfect analogy to sum up the seven key lessons I have learned. I call it the slackliner's mindset.

1) Stay focused
2) Be persistent
3) Build your confidence
4) Find your balance
5) Maintain a positive outlook
6) Be present
7) Learn from successful people

LESSON ONE

STAY FOCUSED

*"Your destiny is to fulfill those things upon which you focus
most intently. So, choose to keep your focus on
that which is truly magnificent, beautiful, uplifting, and joyful.
Your life is always moving toward something."*
—Ralph Marston

Every successful person, whether they are an athlete, a business person, or any other superstar, has one thing in common. They stay focused. Being focused is not just being fixated on something. It is something you are internally driven towards and determined to achieve, no matter what obstacles get in your way. There are six elements to being focused that are part of the slackliner's mindset, which also applies to achieving any goal in life.

1) Have an end goal in mind
2) Create a plan and take action
3) Overcome the wobbles
4) Ditch your excuses
5) Keep your eyes on your goal
6) Stay calm

HAVE AN END GOAL IN MIND

Achievements in life do not happen by accident. People who get results have an end goal in mind. They know where they are and where they want to go. They understand that when you have a goal that you truly believe in, it demands extreme focus. They also know that if you are not reminding yourself of what you are aiming for and the reasons why you want it, it is easy to let life get in the way and distract you.

Slacklining is a perfect example of having an end goal in mind. Your goal is to walk across from one end to the other without falling while keeping your eyes focused on one point at the other end of the line. When you reach the other side, you have achieved your goal. This is easier said than done because until you become a master, it is a sport of wobbling, falling, and getting back up.

If you want to become good at slacklining, or anything new, you must keep your end goal in mind, and you also have to be okay with being a beginner. Even though there is always that initial uncertainty and hesitation that comes from not knowing what you are doing, as long are you are cool with the frustration of wobbling and falling, you will figure it out. The fastest way to overcome that uncertainty and hesitation is to create an action plan.

CREATE A PLAN AND TAKE ACTION

You cannot walk into a gym and grow muscles just by staring at the machines. You must have a picture in your mind of what you want to look like—your end goal— and then create a plan to achieve those results and take action.

Just like building muscles, to go from beginner slackliner to master you have to create a plan to learn and practice the sport, then take action on that plan with your end goal in mind. A plan is nothing more than a set of specific things that you are going to do, as well as when you are going to do them. The plan should be constructed to improve your results so that you can reach your goal. Some examples of a plan for slacklining can include a commitment to practicing a few times a week, for a certain length of time, or watching videos of people who are just beasts at slacklining. It can also include practicing with friends or taking videos of yourself to measure your progress and learn from previous mistakes. Having an end goal in mind, and creating a plan are the first two steps in harnessing the power of focus. The real work is in overcoming the wobbles.

OVERCOME THE WOBBLES

Whenever you start learning something new, there are always going to be obstacles and mini failures that you come across until you figure it out. Failing is part of the learning curve. The key is to be patient as you learn and fail your way to success.

In slacklining, your failures are your wobbles and falls. When you are first walking across a slackline, and you start to wobble, it is difficult to get used to the imbalance. A lot is going on in your brain and body. It is a new experience, and you are recruiting different muscles fibers you have not used before. You have not yet built the right muscle and nerve connections, so your brain is still figuring things out and is adapting. It can be a big learning curve. If your wobbles get super out of control, you will fall. Hopefully, it will be a soft landing.

Every fall is a learning experience—as long as you get back up and try again. Your brain gathers new information from each fall so that it can self-correct the next time you get back on the line. I cannot tell you how many times I have been wobbling and am about to fall off, and then suddenly I can correct and regain my balance. The only way I can do that is because I have already been in that position before that it was becoming familiar.

The learning curve for overcoming the wobbles and falls in slacklining is just like learning to ride a bike on two wheels for the first time, or just starting out skiing. No one is a pro on their first attempt. Everyone falls, and that is where the learning happens. Nobody wants to keep falling. The real trick to dealing with the wobbles and falls is learning how to turn your frustration into motivation and determination to learn and improve quickly.

DITCH YOUR EXCUSES

I am sure most people can relate to having been at a point in their lives where they had been aiming towards something, and then challenges and situations got in their way, leading them to change or even drop their goal completely. Maybe it was taking longer than expected and they lost interest or focus. An unforeseen event may have occurred that limited them from even being able to practice or work towards that goal. It could be a good excuse like they broke a bone or maybe some serious family issues came up. But let us be honest, most of the time when people change or drop a goal, they come up with much smaller excuses to rationalize why they gave up. Then they justify their excuse so that they can feel better about quitting or not having reached their goal.

If you want to achieve anything in life, ditch your excuses and look for reasons why you can succeed instead of reasons you cannot. Excuses are nothing more than rationalizations that you make to justify your behavior or to negate responsibility for undesired results. They are a way of placing blame for your shortcomings on something other than yourself or your choices.

Most people use the same excuses over and over again. The same excuses that they would use for not being able to slackline are probably the same ones they use in other parts of their life. Ditch your excuses and get focused on your goals.

DO NOT TAKE YOUR EYES OFF YOUR GOAL

When walking on a slackline people usually walk heel to toe with their eyes focused at the end of the line. If you know where your foot is, you know where the line is, and you can easily take the next step without looking down. This takes having faith and trusting in yourself that you are taking the right step. Sometimes you may be off balance, and it may not feel right, but the line is there and will support you if you allow it to.

Every step you take on a slackline is a decision to move forward. Sometimes you hesitate before you step, and sometimes you boldly step forward. Even in life, people find themselves in a similar conflict between hesitation and action. Not knowing the right decision is an uncomfortable feeling. You just need to have faith and trust in whatever decision you make. It will not always feel perfect, and not every decision will be a good decision, but things always tend to work out because if you are focused on your end goal, any decision you make is ultimately moving you in the right direction.

Since a slackline is something you walk across, you would think that it is all about your feet and having good balance. But at the core of slacklining, it is all about your eyes and where you focus your attention.

Imagine yourself stepping onto a slackline. As you stand tall with your eyes looking straight ahead at the center of the tree trunk, you find your focus and your balance. You put one foot in front of the other, never taking your eyes off the center of the tree trunk. Your intense focus makes it easy to walk across to the other end of the slackline without falling.

Now, take that same slackline, and instead of staying focused on the center, look down at your feet while trying to walk across. This is what most people do when they are starting out. They think that by looking down, they will know where the line is and that will help them to walk without falling. Looking down seems to make sense, but it is one of the biggest mistakes people make. When you look down at the slackline, you lose focus on the end goal, which causes you to lose your sense of feeling centered and being balanced. The tree was there to guide you and to keep you centered. With your center of gravity thrown off, it doesn't take long before the wobbles cause you to fall.

LESSON ONE: STAY FOCUSED

The visual illusion to overcome is that the slackline always looks centered when you are looking down at it because you are looking from directly above. That is why people want to look at the line instead of straight ahead. However, if you were to look up at the tree at the end of the slackline, you would have a reference as to what your true center is, and your body will self-adjust. Being centered is what the sport is all about. The same thinking applies to life. You cannot achieve something that you are not focused on. If you constantly take your eyes off your goal, or if your focus is not centered on your action plan, you set yourself up for failure.

STAY CALM

Slacklining requires a mentally relaxed focus so that you can keep your thoughts still, remain calm, and stay in touch with your body and mind. When you allow random thoughts to come to your mind that adds stress or gets you out of tune with your body, you can quickly lose focus and fall. You fall because your body follows your mind. When you lose focus and stop paying attention to what you are doing, you wobble, and if you do not know how to refocus quickly, that wobble turns into a fall. The key is to practice staying mentally focused by turning off distracting thoughts so that you can maintain a consistent, relaxed focus.

There is a TED Talk which shares a study about people using a popular cognitive task called *the candle problem* to test the effects of feeling rushed. A group of people are given matches, a box of tacks, and a candle. The task was to attach a lit candle to the wall without getting any wax on the table and to do it as fast as they could. In this particular study, one group was given the task without any incentive to complete it. Another group was given an incentive that the fastest person to complete the task would get some money. The group incentivized with the money was significantly slower than the other group. Why? Because they were rushing so fast, they could not see the whole picture and became sloppy in their approach. The group who was not told to do it fast took a few seconds to look at the whole picture and find a solution.

The lesson from this candle problem applies to slacklining, too. When you rush to get across a slackline, you are not in tune with big picture of getting across calmly and strategically, and so you lose your focus and fall. When faced with any challenge in life, the calmer and more relaxed you are, the easier it is to see the whole picture and come up with a solution. A wobbly, agitated mind will always tumble.

PUTTING THE SIX ELEMENTS TOGETHER

A lot of people are afraid to fall or tumble because they believe that a fall is a failure. I am a big believer in the idea that there are no failures and there are no wrong decisions. Everything that happens is perfect and is exactly what needed to happen. Everything is a learning experience, and every setback is a step forward if you have the right attitude.

Experience is what creates the opportunity for growth, and if you are not growing, you are dying. No matter what you are trying to accomplish in life, if you keep a consistent focus, create a plan and take action on it, overcome your wobbles, and measure your progress, you are on the right track toward hitting your goal. When things get testy, do not look down, stay calm, and you *will* reach your goal with the faith that each step you take is the right step.

A REAL-LIFE EXAMPLE

In my own experience of accomplishing goals, I have learned that it takes the right kind of mindset to both start and finish something. Anyone can set a goal and start to work towards it. Anyone can step onto a slackline. But the real challenge is to make it through the wobbles and keep trying again each time you fall. Not too long ago I worked through a huge wobble that was a major setback toward my goals. Actually, it was more than a wobble. It was a major fall, but it was the slackliner's mindset that got me through it.

I love working out. Lifting weights and looking good is my thing. It is my alone time where I escape and feel the high of my endorphins flowing through my body. In 2016, after spring break, I was in the best condition I had ever been in. I was working my ass off for that spring break trip, and I wanted my body to look its best. Having chiseled abs is one of the trademarks of having a sexy body, and I was committed to getting my sexy on. The following week, after I got back from my spring break trip, I went to the gym and had a great workout. After having not lifted all break, I still managed to crush the workout. I left the gym feeling great. The next day, my lower back was in so much pain, I could not walk. I did not go to school for a week because I could barely even get around my house. It was so bad that I when I sneezed I would collapse on the floor because I could not support myself. I later found out that I had fractured my L5 lower vertebrae. A nerve was rubbing against the fracture causing me the extreme pain.

If you have ever moved around before, you probably have a pretty good idea that your lower back is involved in almost every movement. Knowing

how serious lower back injuries can be, I did not push myself and waited for it to heal. I could not work out for over six months. I was devastated. After all the progress I had made before spring break, I lost it all. I was extremely frustrated with myself at first. However, I knew
I could not reverse anything, and becoming upset would not do me any good. I made the decision to change my attitude about the situation. I still had a long-term goal of being extremely fit and living a healthy lifestyle, and I saw this as an opportunity to learn about the injury and how to prevent it in the future. Recovery is an important part of being an athlete. I knew I was still making progress toward my goal by ensuring I was healing properly.

This injury was a huge setback for me at the time, but it was also a pivotal point in my life. I had taken a hard fall. However, I was determined to get healthy and back into training to achieve my fitness goals—even if
I had to take a long detour of corrective mobility. Once I had reached that point where I accepted what happened and was not going to let it affect the outcome of my goals, I felt free. I no longer felt the pressure I had been putting on myself about the injury. I just kept doing my thing—constantly working on and growing myself by reading books, listening to audios and podcasts, journaling, and setting weekly goals. When the time finally came where I started working out again, I was thrilled to get back into it. I was definitely out of shape based on my personal standards after taking so many months' off, but it motivated me to get off my ass and crush it again.

My new "slackline goal" was getting back in shape, which can be tough after a major injury, but I had achieved the results before, and I knew I had the right mindset to make it happen again. That is the thing with getting back into working out or restarting any goal; it is always difficult to get started again. The task itself may not be difficult, but getting back into the mindset and pushing yourself to actually do it can be a challenge. There are mental blocks to overcome. You have got to figure out how to work it into your routine. Getting started is the easiest time to make excuses and not achieve your goal. This is why people who start working out again every New Year always fall off within the first month. They let the wobbles get in the way of their focus.

LESSON TWO

BE PERSISTENT

*"Ambition is the path to success.
Persistence is the vehicle you arrive in."
— Bill Bradley*

Have you ever felt such a massive inner drive that it did not matter how hard things could get, you would push on anyway? Have you ever felt that incredible feeling that comes from being relentlessly persistent and finally achieving a goal? It is an amazing feeling that is the reward for persistence.

Persistence is that unquenching thirst to achieve a goal no matter what obstacles show up. It is one of the key traits to have when setting out to achieve a goal. To be persistent requires a strong desire to achieve, and a deep, unstoppable belief in your capabilities. Persistence takes patience, practice, and faith to get things done, even when life is pushing back against you.

People who are persistent have a strong enough belief in themselves and their goals to keep them going. They know that they have to patiently pursue their goals, practice to strengthen their weaknesses and keep the faith in themselves that they will get things done.

When a person lacks patience, it overrides their desires and prevents them from being persistent. They do not understand that you cannot rush results. Everything comes at the right time when you are ready and when the conditions are ripe. Only a small percentage of the population exemplifies the true characteristics of someone who is persistent.

Someone who understands the power of persistence, understands and lives by this phrase:

"The teacher will appear when the student is ready."

Persistence is a characteristic of mine that has gotten me to where I am today. One of the best things about this characteristic is that it can be developed. It comes down to how badly you want something. When you truly desire something bad enough, obstacles and setbacks become temporary distractions and detours. Persistence will ensure you get to your destination. For people who want to learn how to develop persistence, I have put together five agreements for getting things done.

- Learn from your mistakes
- It is okay to start over
- Know when to take a break
- Measure your progress
- Adjust your strategy, not your outcome

LEARN FROM YOUR MISTAKES

Slacklining is one of the sports that has ingrained in me the importance of persistence when it comes to learning from your mistakes. If you do not make a habit of learning from your mistakes, if you resist trying over and over again to overcome the wobbles and falls, you will repeatedly fail to reach your goals.

There are no time restraints attached to persistence. Everyone learns and develops it at their own pace. It is a trait that over time will get you where you need to be as long as you are willing to learn from your mistakes.

When I am teaching someone to slackline, I cannot just say, *"Oh you will have this down in an hour."* They might have decent balance and can learn it quickly, or they may be like most people (including me) and suck when they first try it. Most people do not have the patience to learn from their mistakes. They stop trying after the first half hour because they mentally beat themselves up over how they were not good at it. They see someone like me walking across the slackline fairly easily and just decide they cannot do it, but they do not think about the endless hours that I put into practice. Most people want to know how to slackline, but they lack the patience, inner drive, and motivation to learn it. You must be determined and accept that you will make mistakes and have the self-awareness to learn from previous mistakes.

IT IS OKAY TO START OVER

How many times would you give a crawling baby the chance to learn how to walk? Obviously, you would let the baby keep stumbling until it learned how to walk. There is no time limit or number of chances. There is no one telling the baby it cannot walk. It does not have self-doubt about its capability to walk. A baby sees people walking and becomes determined to do so itself. It may cry a little after the first few stumbles, but it does not get upset with starting over. With all its innocence, a baby learning to walk is a model to the importance of the phrase, *"You have to get back up when you fall."*

A *never-give-up attitude* applies to learning anything new. It is the baby approach to learning, and is especially true when slacklining, which requires that you be willing to fall, get back up, and start over continuously.

There is a common perception that having to start over at something means failure. But it does not. Was the baby a failure when it fell? No, because we know that the baby will eventually learn. I recommend applying this same kind of thinking to your own philosophy of life. Develop the mindset that initially failing at something does not make you a failure. It just means that you successfully found a way that it did not work. Just keep starting over until you learn and you will eventually succeed with the right mindset and persistence.

When you are working on accomplishing a goal, initial failures are to be expected. But if you keep failing while trying to accomplish something new, that original excitement and passion that got you started can become diminished. Do not become discouraged. There is real growth that happens when your motivation starts to go away, and you decide to keep pursuing your goal anyway. When you are learning something new, your brain has to create new neuropathways to record what you have learned so that it can do it again. Every time you start over, and with each success, these neuropathways become stronger. Being willing to start over is a must because it wires your brain for success.

MEASURE YOUR PROGRESS

If you want to wire your brain for success, you have to be willing to measure your progress. There are a few ways to measure progress, and they all have their benefits, depending on what you are trying to accomplish. Keeping a journal is my favorite way because I know that the goals I write down are real and I want them to happen.

Other ways of measuring progress are to shoot videos of yourself in action and to learn from watching them. You can also record audios so that you can hear how you come across to others. Best of all, get an accountability partner—someone who you can be accountable towards with your goals so that you stay on track and do not quit. If you do not measure your progress, it is equivalent to taking your eyes off your end goal—which is a sure way to wobble and fall.

Slacklining is a great way to learn the value of measuring your progress because the results are instantaneous. Failing tends to happen quickly. You wobble and then fall. You measure your progress by how quickly you get back up and how much longer you stay on the slackline without falling. Not all goals give you feedback that quickly, but you can learn from this example the importance of keeping track of your progress and applying it to other parts of your life.

Being the gym rat that I am, the best way I can relay the importance of measuring your progress in anything you do, including slacklining, is with the example of building muscle from lifting weights.

It should be a given that the results you want from working out will not happen overnight. Have you ever met someone who wants to get in shape but gets discouraged when they see other people with the results that they want? The desired results are so far from where they currently are that doubt begins to creep in.

I do not think many people understand how many guys hit the gym every single day, lifting heavy weights, taking supplements, eating large meals, and are not seeing that great of results. One of the biggest reasons for this is because they do not measure their progress. They do the same workout routine for months, always starting out their workout with the same lifts, which eventually leads them to reach a plateau in their strength. People who are fit and have noticeable results with their body typically have some way of measuring their progress so that they do not reach a plateau. There are apps for measuring your workouts, or you can just keep track with paper and pencil.

In that first month of January, when people start flocking to the gym for New Year's resolutions, the majority of them quit within their first few weeks. One of the most common reasons for this is because they are not seeing results quickly enough, and they lose focus. People do not measure their progress, so they do not see the small gains. Without seeing the incremental gains they lose the motivation to give themselves enough time to get measurable results.

People get motivated when they see results. What those people who quit early do not realize is that when you first start working out, your initial results are not always easily noticed, but they are there. The key is to build momentum. Small increases in strength stack up and lead to bigger gains. You have to learn to notice the small gains so that you stay positive and motivated. The reality is, everyone is making progress each time they workout. Some people are just not aware of what is happening at the physiological level. When you exercise and recruit muscles, all kinds of metabolic factors are taking place to help fight inflammation, give you energy, increase focus, and even promote better sleep. Working out also helps develop persistence, strength, and self-discipline.

A great way to stay motivated and measure progress is to write down your workouts. Keep track of how many sets, reps, and the amount of weight you lifted. Then, during the next workout, do more than what you did the previous week. It sounds simple, and it is. This process is powerful because the amount of volume in your workouts can always be increased each week. However, majority of people are not keeping track of their workouts and therefore are not pushing themselves hard enough each week. It is very satisfying when you measure your progress and realize that you were stronger and performed better than the previous week. It adds to your motivation to stick with it because you are achieving results even though you may not see physical results in the mirror yet.

Another great way to measure progress that I use is to take progress pictures of your body every few weeks from different angles. At the end of every month, take a new set of pictures and compare it to the ones at the beginning of the month. Do not be shocked when you are wondering who that sexy person is. Keep up the good work!

Measuring progress is not just for fitness. You should measure it in all areas of your life. Whether it is fitness, slacklining, school, or any skill you are working on, always pay attention to where you started. It is easy to beat yourself up and not think you are making progress when you look at short-term results. But when you keep track, you can see how your small achievements stack up, leading to big results.

ADJUST YOUR STRATEGY, NOT YOUR OUTCOME

I think I have been pretty clear on the need to be persistent and measure your progress. But if what you are doing is not getting the results you want, and you are not getting closer to your goal, you may be persistent but have the wrong strategy. If you are trying to learn how to walk on a slackline while wearing high heels, no matter how many times you practice, you may never get it figured out. If you are trying to build muscle and are eating a restricted diet, getting results is going to be close to impossible.

When your results do not match your effort, you need to become more aware of what is or is not working through the feedback of your results. When what you are doing is no longer working, adjust your strategy, but stay focused on your outcome.

Every time you experience a wobble on a slackline, it may be a wobble you have felt before and can correct it. Or, it may be one you have not dealt with before. Either way, learn from the wobble. As long as you are open to learning from the wobble, you can adjust your strategy until you can walk steadily.

I am sure you have experienced a situation where you felt a wobble in your life and did nothing to change or learn from it. It is like getting a speeding ticket. For those next couple days you may be a more careful driver, but soon enough you are speeding again. What was the lesson we learned from getting that speeding ticket? Well, obviously, not to get caught. Just kidding! I am not supporting speeding. One speeding ticket is just a small wobble. Most do not learn from it or change their behavior. But when someone gets a couple of speeding tickets and has had to pay fines, take classes, and deal with everyone's favorite place—court—a change in driving strategy tends to take place. Whether that be driving slower or buying a radar detector, the change in strategy is up to you.

Learn from your small wobbles before they become big. A slight change in behavior or shift in what you are doing now could prevent some serious unwanted consequences down the road. Learning from your mistakes allows you to make the necessary changes to your strategy and shapes you into who you are.

I have done some pretty stupid things in my life, many that I am not proud of. But at the end of the day, those mistakes were the lessons I needed to learn. They made me into the person I am today. Sometimes you learn what to do by learning what *not* to do.

We all experience setbacks and make mistakes. Learning how to adjust your strategy is what will take you farther in life with anything you do. Michael Jordan, Les Brown, Gary Vaynerchuk, and so many other great leaders and role models have proven what persistence can do. They have all learned how to measure their progress and adjust their strategy when their results do not match their desired outcome. If you want results, you must stay after it. Developing the mental sharpness to know when it is time to adjust your strategy is a characteristic that will build confidence, and flow into all areas of life. Take this lesson to heart; I promise it can only benefit you.

LESSON THREE

BUILD YOUR CONFIDENCE

"Belief in oneself is incredibly infectious. It generates momentum, the collective force of which far outweighs any kernel of self-doubt that may creep in."
— Aimee Mullins

Staying focused and being persistent is the beginning of the slackliner's mindset. Having confidence in yourself is what takes you from being a beginner to being a badass slacker. Confidence is everything. It effects the actions you take, the results you get, and the people you allow into your life.

Even though there a lot of people who have confidence in themselves and their ability to tackle any new challenge, there are plenty of people who lack confidence, and it gets in the way of anything new that they try to accomplish. This lack of confidence can show up as being too hard of a critic of yourself or caring too much about what other people think of you. This is especially true in high school, which is a crucial time for building confidence because everyone wants to fit in and be accepted. No one wants to be the outsider or the oddball who is made fun of by others. Because of this, kids act differently around their classmates than who they truly are—just to be liked by them. I have witnessed this firsthand and can say I am guilty of this act myself. I never really had a hard time making friends or fitting in. Interacting with other people and making friends is something I love to do. But that doesn't mean I never went through problems with self-confidence.

I originally started working out because I did not want to be a small kid and wanted to look good for the ladies. Most guys can relate. But for my self-confidence and working out, it was a strange relationship. I fell in love with the pump and how working out made me feel. I began to start making some good progress gaining size and strength. I went through a stage where I would wear shirts with cut-off sleeves so I could show off my cannons. But I soon realized after seeing other bigger guys in the gym that I was just child's play. I was determined to get big like these other guys. But as I continued to see shredded guys all over the internet, my self-confidence about how I looked began to dwindle.

Even though I was among the top athletes in my class and had a lot of size compared to most, I did not have much confidence in myself about my appearance. I was too busy comparing myself to others instead of comparing myself to me. I dealt with this confidence issue in college, too, until I finally just said, *"Fuck it. I love myself for who I am. I do not care what other people think or how I compare to other guys. The only person I am trying to be better than, is me."*

This brings me back to slacklining. One of the things that I love about slacklining is that when you step on the slackline, there is no judging. The slackline does not care about your faults. It is only there to support you. You are responsible for how quickly and easily you walk across.

How you see yourself and how your life turns out is totally up to you. It does not matter if you had a shitty or kickass childhood. You are responsible for creating the person you want to become.

If you are not happy with your life and you want to make changes, work on building up your confidence, which is something I have done for myself many times. My method for building confidence can be chunked down into six benchmarks to building confidence.

- Change your story
- Take inventory of your strengths
- Set yourself up to win
- Believe in yourself
- Take risks
- Celebrate small victories

CHANGE YOUR STORY

Have you ever noticed that the difference between lucky people and unlucky people is the story they are telling themselves? A lucky person believes and thinks of themselves as being lucky. An unlucky person is always talking about how unlucky they are, and they believe they are unlucky.

Who you become is directly linked to the story you believe about yourself. Your story is a collection of beliefs you have accumulated about yourself and the events in your life. It is made up of the thoughts you tend to tell yourself repeatedly. Your thoughts can make you feel confident or give you low self-esteem. They can project you forward or hold you back. How you perceive yourself determines how you make decisions. What kind of story are you telling yourself? Are you in charge of your life, or is your story holding you back? Does your story allow you to feel confident and believe in yourself, or does it make you shrink and feel powerless? Does your story prevent you from doing things, or does it motivate you?

If you are serious about building confidence, you have to take the time to identify your story, and then change your thoughts to match your new story. Thoughts are one of the few things you have complete control over. By changing your thoughts, you alter your story. If your story was once holding you back, you can create a new story that propels you forward.

Your story affects every part of your life. Slacklining is all about your story. At first, most peoples' story about their slacklining experience is that they sucked. This may be true at first, but it is not the right attitude to maintain, and it does not have to be the final result. If they truly believe that they suck, they throw up a big mental block that makes it next to impossible to learn. A better story would be, *"I suck at slacklining right now, but I know I can figure this out and make it happen."* It takes conscious effort to change your story and give yourself supportive thoughts when you otherwise want to complain and quit. Every time you create a winning belief in your story, it becomes easier to get a result and builds self-confidence.

The story you tell yourself creates your reality. It is easy to come up with reasons why things cannot or will not work or to justify excuses. When you change your belief, your actions tend to follow. If you desire better results, you are going to have to get better beliefs and create a better story.

TAKE INVENTORY OF YOUR STRENGTHS

Developing better beliefs starts with taking inventory of your strengths. Many people have a habit of focusing on what is wrong with them, which is why so many people lack confidence.

People with confidence know their strengths, and they build upon them by giving themselves challenges that make them stronger and more confident. When you develop confidence in one part of your life, you can lean on that confidence and use the same mindset to build better beliefs and confidence in other situations. One of the fastest ways to get better beliefs and build confidence is to set yourself up to win.

Developing better beliefs starts with taking inventory of your strengths. Focusing on your faults or worrying about potential problems is no fun. With a slight change in how you think about yourself, it will dramatically increase how you feel.

A simple shift I made in my thinking was changing a question I was asking myself. I had noticed that in the evenings when I got home and looked at my board of objectives for that day, I would ask myself,

What did I not get done today?

I always found answers, and it was sucking a lot of energy out of me. I saw this pattern and came up with a new question.

What did I accomplish today?

This new question forced me to think of my strengths and what I did accomplish that day, and made me feel a whole lot better about myself.

Asking yourself positive questions when you look back on your day will magnify your strengths. Knowing your strengths and building upon them is a must if you want to build confidence and believe in yourself.

SET YOURSELF UP TO WIN

Confidence is the main ingredient to success, especially with slacklining. Most people quit too soon because they do not believe in themselves.

When teaching someone how to slackline, I set them up to win. Instead of focusing on the entire slackline and the intimidation of probably falling, I have them focus on small wins. If they can walk two steps, then that is great! We celebrate those two steps and aim for three steps on the next try. Small wins added together creates massive momentum. This keeps confidence high during each attempt with a determination to do better than before.

People naturally tend to perform their best when they feel confident in themselves. A strong enough belief can do just about anything. Set yourself up to win using small victories to create momentum.

BELIEVE IN YOURSELF

For a lot of people, believing in themselves is not the easiest thing. There are always times when life gets rough, and you lose some belief in yourself. Rely on friends who believe in you or are at least nice enough to encourage you to leverage their belief into your own. Having friends who support you is very powerful when it comes to believing in yourself. That

LESSON THREE: Build Your Confidence

is why it is important to keep people in your life who build you up and encourage you. They help you embrace that belief that lies within you.

Not only should you be aware of surrounding yourself with uplifting people, but also be aware of avoiding the negative energy suckers. These people can rob you of your beliefs and destroy everything you are working hard to build if you let them. They are usually quick to judge and constantly voice their opinions. With practice, I managed to block out their negativity and stick to my own beliefs. You can, too.

If you do not have a good support system and/or live in a toxic environment, you will be okay if you develop a strong belief in yourself. If you can, make changes in your life so that you can get rid of the energy suckers and bring higher quality people into your life. Use the slackliner's mindset and the techniques in this book if you need help raising belief in yourself.

TAKE RISKS

When some people hear the word "risk," they get nervous. Others get excited. Risk is involved in just about anything you do. Walking across a slackline comes with its own risk. It may not be a big risk because it is only a couple of feet off the ground, but for a new person, it can seem big. Everyone has their level of comfort with how much risk they are willing to take. Personally, I am pretty risky. Whether it be jumping off cliffs, pursuing huge goals, or putting money down on an investment, the risk is usually worth the reward. Sometimes the reward is a big win, and sometimes it is a life lesson.

Taking risks is exciting. If a deal goes through in my favor, I could make a killing. That possibility is usually enough for me. Sure, I could lose on the deal. But it would not kill me. Losing money or losing your life is a big difference.

I take most risks as long as I do not have a good chance of dying. I am motivated by risk because one of my biggest fears is regret. I take risks because I am scared that if I do not, I will regret the missed opportunity. Nobody likes regret. Taking risks can also raise confidence if all goes well. Most of the time, if you are presented with a risky opportunity, you are not going to feel super confident. But you will feel highly confident and super excited if that risk plays out in your favor. Take risks with whatever you feel comfortable with, or even a bit uncomfortable if it forces you to grow. Just keep focused on the positive side of what you could gain if you succeed, and look for the win if you lose.

CELEBRATE SMALL VICTORIES

There is a lot to gain from taking risks and celebrating small victories. It builds your confidence and raises your energy. For a long time, I would write on my whiteboard a bunch of things I wanted to get done that day. Sometimes I would not be able to cross everything off the list by the end of the day. Things would come up, or I was not realistic about the amount of time everything would take. I would end my day feeling disappointed in myself because I did not achieve everything I said I would.

A great friend of mine who I call Super Dave told me I needed to celebrate my small victories. Instead of writing down a bunch of things to do that day, I should write down just a few of the most important things to get done and do them. This was a big deal for me. It did not mean I could not get other things done that day. In fact, I often do a lot more than is written on my board. But when I complete my most important tasks and cross them off, I feel a great sense of accomplishment. If I still have time left over I can work on other tasks at hand that were not a priority for that day.

Setting priorities changed my way of thinking because I would no longer get overwhelmed. A key component to writing down the major tasks for the day is deciding what you are going to do when they are completed. Before you jump to the next task, you need to celebrate. Get yourself pumped up. Not only does this give you the energy you need for the next task, but it is activating the pleasure center of your brain. With consistency, your brain will start to crave that pleasure. Making you more productive and confident.

***

IT WORKED FOR ME

For a long time, I had been telling myself that people would not buy a fitness program from me. I made up stories that other people were better than me, knew more information, or had a bigger following than me. Fortunately, some friends of mine told me I just needed to change my story. The reality is that there was nothing stopping anyone from buying a program from me other than my limiting beliefs. I have been fortunate enough to connect and learn from some of the best, which has expanded my knowledge beyond what most personal trainers know. This has transitioned me to take more of a holistic approach when helping people with their fitness and health goals. All I needed to do was to change my story and have confidence in myself that I could do it. My friends were right. Ever since I changed my mindset, I started getting clients.

I set myself up to win by starting with my friends and giving them a "friend discount." Gaining new clients was a big win. I believed in myself and took the risk to go for it. Even if I would have failed or embarrassed myself, in the end, I found myself to be celebrating a lot of victories.

Building confidence was the missing link that was holding me back. When I changed my story and focused on my strengths, everything else changed.

LESSON FOUR

FIND YOUR BALANCE

"No person, no place, and no-thing has any power over us, for 'we' are the only thinkers in our mind. When we create peace and harmony and balance in our minds, we will find it in our lives."
—*Louise L. Hay*

Have you ever gotten to the point where you were so caught up in all the things going on in your life that all of a sudden, something just hit you, and you were like, *"Damn, I need a break"?* You might have been burnt out from work and in need of a vacation or just needed to take a break from stress. Most of us have been there before. We all need some breaks in our lives to refresh our mind and body, reduce stress, increase happiness, and find that inner balance.

Everyone deserves to be happy, and it goes hand in hand with living a balanced life. If work or school takes away from your health, you might get sick and become unhappy. If you spend too much time partying and miss out on opportunities or don't get work done, you might become unhappy about your bank account. On the contrary, if you are making good money but never have social time with friends, you may not be as happy as you want. For me, the ultimate goal in life is to be in a constant state of happiness. Part of achieving that is finding balance in your daily life.

For me, living a balanced life is keeping things dynamic and doing what feels right. There is no right way to live a balanced life. Everyone has different interests and hobbies. But mixing things up so you are not stuck in the same pattern is what I find keeps life fun and makes me feel balanced.

Finding balance can be a real struggle. It is a battle between all of your responsibilities and commitments and all the fun stuff that you want to do. But it does not have to be a difficult battle. No matter what you are doing, there are four simple steps to finding a balance that you can easily apply at any time of day.

- Breathe and chill
- Take time for yourself
- Expand your awareness
- Listen to feedback

BREATHE AND CHILL

Learning how to use your breath to relax and find balance is one of the easiest things to do. Use your imagination for a moment and visualize yourself getting ready to step onto a slackline. Before you step up onto the line, take a deep breath, exhale slowly, and chill. Quiet your thoughts and allow yourself to become mentally relaxed. This will help with your concentration, relax your body, and bring oxygen into your brain, helping you to focus. You are now ready to step onto the slackline without worry or tension.

Using this breathe-and-chill technique is very effective. The mind thinks more clearly when it is relaxed and fully oxygenated, and the body is much stronger and more responsive.

When you breathe, you are using the same core muscles that you use when finding your balance on a slackline. Your core muscles provide stability for your body. When you start to wobble on the slackline, your core muscles tighten in an attempt to help you regain balance, and your breathing briefly stops or becomes shallow. When I start to wobble, the only thoughts passing through my mind are about trying not to fall. After fighting the battle of getting balanced again, I always take a deep breath to regain focus. That calming breath brings everything back into focus and under my control.

Breathing is the cure for the wobbles. Life's wobbles are the challenges that throw you out of balance. You may have to grind for a test or a project deadline. You may be working non-stop, or taking care of the family. During times like these make sure you take time to breathe and get centered again. I discovered that part of finding balance was being aware of when I needed to grind shit out, and when I needed to take a breather and chill.

I use this breathe-and-chill technique all the time for self-reflection. I feel more clear-headed and have a better time planning what I need to do to improve my life when I relax and breathe. The next time you get stressed or become unbalanced, take the time to slow down and breathe. It helps to keep balance in your life and to keep you happy.

TAKE TIME FOR YOURSELF

If life ever overpowers you, there is no one else that can help you regain peace than you. I have noticed for myself how important it is to have a way to get back to feeling a sense of peace and balance. I do this by keeping an adventurous attitude and making a habit of taking time for myself. College can be very stressful and can get so busy that I forget to give some time to myself. Often I will get to a point where I just need to chill and get outside and hit the slackline. It is almost healing for me. I love it because it allows me to be outside and reinforces tons of life lessons.

I also love going on hikes and doing activities with friends as a way to take time for myself. When you do something fun, it changes your energy and gives you feelings of happiness. Think about a time when you went on a vacation, and you came back home pumped up. Those fun experiences let you enjoy life and give you reasons to be grateful. These are the kind of feelings and energy we need in our lives. If you are not giving some time for yourself to have fun, I suggest you start right now. Finding time by yourself or with friends to do things you enjoy is essential for keeping balance.

EXPAND YOUR AWARENESS

A big part of finding your balance is expanding your awareness about life so that you can connect with new ways to be happy and making those things a part of your lifestyle.

Happiness and having a balanced and fulfilled life is my long-term end game. It is a priority for me and is what keeps me motivated. I have learned the importance of doing the things that make me happy because when I am happy, I am more focused and productive. One of the things I love the most is to travel. I have been fortunate enough to see many places around the world and will continue to do so throughout my life.

Seeing different cultures, especially third-world countries, and the way people live has been very humbling. It has broadened my perspective of humanity and has made me appreciate my life so much more.

One thing I have taken away from visiting underdeveloped countries is how the people always seem happy. There seems to be more balance in their life. They seem to place more significance and time on intrinsic values—being close to friends and family, rather than the extrinsic values of attaining worldly status and material possessions. They do not spend their lives checking social media, watching TV shows and movies, or sitting at a desk staring at a computer screen. They may be deprived of many of our luxuries and technological advances, but they enjoy authentic human connection.

I just recently came back from a two-week trip to Peru and Ecuador. Peru is a very poor country. Over 60% of the Peruvian citizens make less than $10 a day. In the marketplace, there are tons of little shops about the size of a cubicle, all with the same products. However, these people still get by. They are extremely nice people, always waving and smiling. They are friends with their neighbors and are grateful for what they have. This ambitious, constant hustle to make ends meet with an amazing attitude is truly inspiring.

If you have the opportunity to travel somewhere, do it. Experiencing another culture and other parts of the world is priceless and can only add value to your life. You will learn a lot about yourself and will help you stay focused on your long-term goals, because it teaches you the value of life. I find myself doing a lot of self-reflection during and after my travels. No matter where I go or what I do, I usually end up with a new and different perspective of life, based on my experiences from where I have visited.

I give everyone the same challenge I have given myself. This world is amazing. Do what you can to find or create an opportunity to see as much as you can of this planet. Who knows how long it will be around? I am grateful that in this day and age, we can see so much of this world through the use of the internet. It is incredible that we can see pictures and videos of the entire world from the palm of our hand. But nothing is more enriching for your heart and soul than when you go to those places in person, experience the culture, and get a real understanding of what some of this world has to offer.

For me, traveling is a big part of the slackliner's mindset. Sometimes you have to disconnect to reconnect. Traveling allows me to disconnect from my current reality and keep balance in my life, giving me relief from the stresses and challenges of daily living. Traveling gives me something to look forward to as well. Every time I return home after an adventure, it motivates me to stay focused on my goals so that I can create the time and money to do it again. I know that when I travel, I will always be learning and growing, which is what I love to do.

I am following the advice that I was given. The first part was to travel while you are young and do crazy things before you have too much responsibility and a family that depends on you. The second part was to stay focused and work hard now to enjoy benefits later. It is all a balance.

LISTEN TO FEEDBACK

If living a balanced life is so important, why does it seem like so many people are out of balance? A lot of people live an unbalanced life and are in a constant state of high stress because they have been doing it for so long that they think it is normal. How do you recognize the need for balance when you do not know you need it? The answer is pretty simple. You have to become self-aware of the conditions of your life and listen to the feedback that your life is giving you.

With slacklining, feedback is instantaneous. If you are off balance, you feel it because you start to wobble. If you lean from one side to the other to correct your balance, the slackline will give you the feedback to let you know if you are regaining balance, or if you need to adjust accordingly. The key is to recognize and pay attention to the feedback you are receiving so that you can make the correct adjustments.

In life, the easiest way to tell if you are out of balance is to pay attention to your feelings. Listening to your feelings will tell you what you are thinking about and focusing on. Your thoughts determine your feelings, and your feelings will drive your actions. If something does not feel right or is causing you stress, ask yourself what it is that is causing those feelings. By asking self-reflective questions about your feelings, you can get in the habit of becoming self-aware of the conditions of your life.

It is best to become aware of when you are falling out of balance. You want to develop a habit of recognizing the situations that affect your emotions in a good way or bad way. If something makes you feel good and makes you happy and fulfilled, then it will add to you feeling balanced. Do more of the good things and less of the bad things. The famous Dr. Seuss said it perfectly.

> "You have brains in your head. You have feet in your shoes.
> You can steer yourself any direction you choose."

When it comes to your body and your health, you have to pay attention to whatever makes you feel healthy and strong, or shitty and weak. Your body is always giving you the feedback of whether or not you are in or out of balance based on how you physically feel.

Have you ever been sitting at a computer for hours or doing work at a desk for an extended period and get cramps or intense stiffness in your back or neck? This happens because it is not natural for the body to hunch over like that. The cramps are feedback from your body that you need to take a break, move around, and stretch. The body needs movement. It is not designed to stay in one place forever.

The same applies to life. Sometimes events happen that force you to move and change. This is a dynamic universe that does not like when things remain the same. If you do not pay attention to the feedback that life is giving you about the need for change, negative emotions and energy begin to stack up throughout your body. This buildup of negativity never leads anywhere good and can eventually get released through injury, illness, or disease, or through some form of mental or emotional breakdown.

Finding balance does not happen instantly. It takes some time to figure out your balance and what works for you. I have learned that balance comes with practice. You have to plan it into your life. Set up regular times to take a break from your busy day-to-day life and enjoy time with friends or get out into nature.

Do not underestimate the healing power of taking a physical and mental break, especially through being in nature. Giving yourself time and space away from your daily life relieves stress and allows your mind to take a break from the conditions of your life.

Finding balance in your life is a choice.
- Take some depth breaths to stay calm and relieve any stress
- Take time for yourself every day doing what makes you happy
- Stay focused on your end game
- Listen to the feedback that life is giving you

Enjoy your balance!

LESSON FIVE

MAINTAIN A POSITIVE OUTLOOK

"Attitude is a choice. Happiness is a choice. Optimism is a choice. Kindness is a choice. Giving is a choice. Respect is a choice. Whatever choice you make makes you. Choose wisely."
— Roy T. Bennett

Did you know that how you look at a situation is a choice? You can choose to be either optimistic or pessimistic. People who are optimistic have positive expectations and know how to make the best out of anything that happens. Those who are pessimistic have negative expectations and look for faults. They justify their shortcomings and failures and tend to be the people who think of themselves as unlucky and always have stories to prove it. Whichever person you are, your results will always match up with your expectations and beliefs.

Maintaining a positive outlook is also a big part of the slackliner's mindset. It is very difficult to make it all the way across a slackline if your mind is full of negative thoughts, and you are worried about falling. Falling does not make you a failure when you have a positive outlook because you see each fall as a way to learn and improve. For people who want to develop that winning edge of the slackliner's mindset, there are three things you can do to develop and maintain a positive outlook.

- Look for the win in everything
- Have a can-do attitude
- Do not worry about other people's opinions (OPOs)

LOOK FOR THE WIN IN EVERYTHING

I have always been a very positive and optimistic guy, and this has served my life for the better. Immersing myself in personal development has pushed me forward into becoming a master of positivity. No matter what happens in my life, I am always looking for the benefits. It has become a subconscious habit of mine to look for the best in everything. Even a bad event or situation can be looked at positively. My core belief is, *"If anything bad happens, it is for the better, and something good will come out of it."*

Not too long ago, I was pulled over for going 30 miles over the speed limit. You could say it was a bad situation and I was freaking out. I had no excuse and was given a ticket. I was pissed at myself, but I told myself that somehow it would work out to my ultimate advantage. I also told myself it was supposed to happen to prevent me from getting into an accident. Just a slight change in thinking makes all the difference for how you feel.

I did not worry about the ticket up until my court date, and even then, I still told myself things would ultimately work out for the best, and they did. I was given the option to have the ticket dropped down to one point if I took a driving safety class for a small fee. You could say I was happy with that. My next court date ended up being scheduled on a Wednesday right in between two exams I had that day. I rescheduled those exams an extra two days later. It absolutely saved my ass, since I was already pretty far behind in class.

When you look for the win in everything that happens to you, you will find it because you will always come up with an answer to your questions. If you want to stay consistently positive, you have to ask yourself the right questions. If you just experienced a bad event, instead of asking yourself, *"Why me?"* or *"Why does this shit always happen to me?,"* ask what you can learn from it or what good can come out of it. With the right question, you will find the win in everything.

HAVE A CAN-DO ATTITUDE

Remember my story of injuring my back and not being able to work out for over six months? There is more to this story. After my back healed, I tapped into a can-do attitude mindset and started working out again. A couple of months went by and I was starting to get strong again. I gained all my strength back from the time I originally hurt my back. Things were good, and I was getting serious in the gym again. One day I was working out my legs and feeling great. I loaded up the weight on the hack squat machine and on my second set, I squatted down only to feel a pop in my lower back in the exact spot I had the previous injury. I collapsed to the ground in horrible pain. Everything I had just gone through the year before was flashing through my mind. Luckily, there was enough adrenaline pumping through my body that I was able to get my ass off the floor, walk out of the gym and go home.

At first, my re-injury seemed like a bad situation for me. Even though the pain was not as bad as the first time, it did put me out of commission. I was devastated not to be able to work out again. I was determined not to let this affect me, and I changed my attitude to focus on where I was going to find the win and how to fix this situation.

Being well-educated in fitness and kinesiology, I knew it was my biomechanics that was causing problems. The injury led me to deep research about injuries and how they relate to functional movement.

I found myself learning all kinds of amazing information that I could use to help my clients. I learned that I had very tight hips and hamstrings that were pulling hard on my spine. It turns out that most people who experience lower back pain are not aware that the pain is not coming from their lower back. There are other muscles that are too tight that are causing the pain.

From this injury, I was led to a path that has now expanded my awareness around all kinds of mobility issues and injuries. Even though this back injury was at first a negative situation, without an attitude and belief that I could fix the problem, I would never have learned about the holistic approach to mobility. My new awareness led me to find not only how to cure myself and prevent the injury, but how I could integrate this holistic approach into training my clients.

DO NOT WORRY ABOUT OTHER PEOPLE'S OPINIONS

Have you ever noticed that some people are always willing to give their opinion about everything, even things that they know little or nothing about? And then there are those people who tell others about their difficulties and failures and why things did not work. They want you to use their failures as a reason to not attempt or try. How would you ever know if you could slackline if you let someone talk you out of it who had quit? How could you ever learn anything new if you always got your advice from people who quit or failed, or never achieved the results you desire for yourself?

The slackliner's mindset answers these questions. It comes down to raising your standards about the people you allow in your life. True slackliners, the ones who know how to learn and improve their game, have one badass standard:

Do not worry about other people's opinions.

All too often, people who are close to us, usually friends or family, love to give their unsolicited opinion about whatever we are doing. Even though they have good intentions, a lot of times those opinions suck because they are negative and do nothing beneficial to help us move forward. To combat these disruptive opinions, you need to develop discernment about whose opinions you listen to. You also need to develop the insight to immediately recognize negativity so that you can exercise your willpower and allow that negativity to slide right by you. If you do not develop the discernment or insight, those opinions can slowly sneak into your mind and disrupt your confidence. It is okay to actively listen to what other people are saying, but you do not always have to agree. It is up to you to stay positive and focused on your goals and to take guidance from the right people.

No matter whose opinion you listen to, you are the creator of your destiny. The only opinion that matters is your own. The highest and best standard is to develop your opinions by listening to the wisdom and insights of those who have the results you want. Just about every personal success story talks about people who had been told that they could not achieve their goal. The ones who chose not to listen to the haters and believed in themselves are the ones who became successful.

***

Maintaining a positive outlook on life has greatly impacted my life for the better. I used to listen to a lot of people's opinions, regardless of their results. Now I only seek advice and feedback from reliable and trusted sources. Since discovering how to simply change my thoughts and attitude, I am now in control of my outlook on life. Nobody likes feeling upset, down on themselves, or even angry, so developing a positive mindset is a tool that can be used to avoid those feelings and give you the feelings you truly want.

LESSON SIX

LIVE IN THE MOMENT

*"The secret of health for both mind and body is not to mourn for the past,
worry about the future, or anticipate troubles,
but to live in the present moment wisely and earnestly."*
— *Buddha*

If you were to look at how you live your life, how often is it that you are truly living in the present moment? With all of today's mobile technology, we are constantly being bombarded with notifications and information that keep our minds distracted from the here and now. Our brains are constantly running thoughts about the past and future.

The media has the attention of the population hooked, and they use their power and influence to keep everyone living in fear about the next big unknown that can rob your health or happiness. At the same time, TV programs and businesses are also fighting for your attention. They are constantly marketing to you in order to keep their brands in your head so that you remain a loyal consumer of their products.

All of this attention-grabbing is extremely hard to avoid, and it can be all-consuming. It is rare that we put those distractions aside so that we can live in the moment and be at peace with ourselves.

I read a popular book called *The Power of Now* by Eckhart Tolle, which talks about living in the moment. I related to it so well that his message changed my life significantly. Here is a great quote from Tolle that sums up what I learned from him.

*"Unease, anxiety, tension, stress, worry—all forms of fear
—are caused by too much future, and not enough presence.
Guilt, regret, resentment, grievances, sadness, bitterness, and all forms of
non-forgiveness are caused by too much past, and not enough presence."*

I connected with this statement because I realized that I had been misguided about my perception of time. A big portion of personal development and working on yourself is having goals to aim toward in the future. In my case, I was always focused on the future, constantly anticipating what was to come. Tolle identified a great point in saying that people are not living in the present, but rather the past and future. I was living primarily in the future and was not fully aware of the present moment. The fact is, the present and the future are connected, but the past is not. The reason is because you cannot change the past, and the present moment does not affect the past like it affects the future. What you do now at this moment creates your future.

There were times when I lived in the present moment without thinking about it, but it was not my norm. Those times were when I was doing activities I loved—things like hiking, traveling, snowboarding, skating, and of course, slacklining. It is much easier to live in the present when you are doing things you love. For me, it is when I am in nature; something about it pulls me into the moment.

Slacklining also brings me into the moment. When I go set up my slackline, either by myself or with friends, I challenge myself to live in the moment. As soon as my foot touches the line, all distractions melt away, and I become fully present and focused.

Now that slacklining is a regular part of my life, and I have gotten good at it, I realize that I have five reference points that help me live in the moment.

- Take one step at a time
- Do not dwell on your problems
- Urgent vs. important
- Change your perspective
- Just ask

TAKE ONE STEP AT A TIME

When you are working on attaining a goal or creating something, you have to go at it one step at a time. This may seem obvious, but you would be surprised how many people try to skip ahead while trying to do something. Skipping steps and overlooking them can come back to haunt you. Earlier in this book, I talked about the need to create a plan and act on that plan.

You cannot do the last step first; it takes a progression of small steps that happen in sequence for the attainment of a goal or desire.

When slacklining, taking one step at a time is the key to success. As important as it is to focus on the goal of getting to the other end of the slackline without falling, it is just as important to be aware of where you currently are in the present moment. You cannot take one step at a time if your mind is wandering all over the place. As you listen to the feedback that your body is giving you to stay balanced, you will naturally take your next step when you feel aligned and centered. If you take a step while wobbling, you are likely to throw yourself completely out of balance and then fall. All your power lies in the current moment and being aware when it is okay to take the next step. Everything that occurs in life happens in the current moment. Tolle refers to it as the *Now*.

When I started to realize the importance of taking one step at a time, I also discovered that the power of the present moment is under my control. I then began to put that awareness and intention into everything I did. When I go to the gym, I am there to work out. Nothing else. My focus is on that mind-muscle connection and giving my full attention to each rep, one at a time. Any other bad or unnecessary thoughts going on in my mind are left outside the gym door because all they do is cause me to have a workout that is not my best. How can anyone expect to do their best at something if their mind is scattered with all kinds of thoughts? The way I un-scatter my mind is through that breathe-and-chill exercise. I take a deep breath and exhale slowly. This calms my body and thoughts so I can direct my focus on taking one step at a time.

DO NOT DWELL ON YOUR PROBLEMS

We all know of people who continuously dwell on all the problems going on in their life. When people dwell on their problems, they are just re-creating each problem in their head and keeping it alive, often making it worse than it is. It is okay to acknowledge and be aware of your problems. But it makes a whole lot more sense to put all your energy and attention into finding or creating solutions.

When you dwell on your problems, you are not living in the moment. Just because someone might be in a problematic situation does not mean it is always a problem. Here is what I mean: if you are having a relationship problem, and you are out at a bar drinking a beer, telling a friend of this "problem" you have, you are making it a problem at that moment. But you do not have a problem at that moment because you are at a bar with a friend. You are making it a problem at that moment because you brought the problem to the bar and are giving it life by talking about it. If you took that same moment and focused on finding a solution, you would no longer have a problem. If your friend is not someone who can help you solve the problem, then talking about it with the wrong person only makes the problem bigger. I understand situations when you want to talk with a friend just to get it off your chest, but what does not make sense is the amount of time and attention people give to these negative emotions. It is as if people like the attention they get when they talk about their problems.

I have seen so many people fall victim to this habit of always talking about their problems, and they do not see how self-destructive it is. There needs to be a switch in their mindset and way of thinking in order to create a change in their life. The switch needs to be to learn how to live in the moment because all solutions are found in the here and now, not in the past.

You will never be able to learn to slackline if all you do is talk about how horrible it is to wobble and fall. Similarly, you will never be able to take the next step forward if your eyes are firmly focused behind you. You do not drive a car while looking in the rear-view mirror, and you do not aim toward a goal by focusing on prior mishaps and failures. It is great to learn from the past, but you do not have to live there.

URGENT OR IMPORTANT

Part of living in the moment is knowing when to respond to something. If being present requires you to let go of distractions, how do you decide what gets your attention? How do you just let everything else go when you have serious issues going on in your life?

What I have learned is that you have to set priorities of what deserves your attention. You have to determine if things are urgent *or* important, or urgent *and* important.

Once you learn how to set your priorities of what you will focus on, it just takes practice to learn how to tune out of things that do not demand your attention right away so that you can focus on what matters most.

From a slackliner's point of view, there is only one perspective that successfully gets you across the slackline—urgent *and* important. When things are urgent and important, they get you focused and keep you in the here and now.

CHANGE YOUR PERSPECTIVE

Another thing I have grown to appreciate about living in the present moment is how much my perspective has changed. I am much more observant. I usually skateboard to class with my headphones on and miss out on what daily life has to offer. When it snows or rains, however, I walk to class. It is interesting how much more of life I notice and appreciate when I walk. Much of what I see would have been passed by on my skateboard.

There have been a few days where I was taking the bus or walking to class, and I forgot my headphones. Every time I did this, I was not able to listen to my music. Instead, I always found myself interacting with other people, including people I had never met before. It showed me an aspect of Fort Collins I had not yet experienced. I realized that whether it be music or your thoughts, anything occupying your mind can prevent you from living and enjoying the moment.

Slacklining has been one of my best teachers for knowing how to change perspective. When you lose your balance and start to wobble, if you want to regain balance, you have to change your perspective and listen to all the feedback coming to you from the slackline. Maintaining that balanced perspective takes a constant state of awareness and presence. It can be a challenge for a lot of people, but learning how to control your perspective gives you control of your outcomes and situations.

When you understand that everything happens in the current moment, you discover the power that is unleashed when you know how to change your perspective from the past or future to the here and now. When you can intentionally change your perspective on-demand, you will come across amazing people and find yourself being presented with new opportunities and information. I have had so many phenomenal experiences that have stemmed from just going with the flow in the present moment. Change your perspective to having your awareness and presence in the moment for a few days, and see how you feel. It will not disappoint you.

JUST ASK

Part of living in the moment is loving and embracing the people that are in your life right now and seeing them as resources to help you build your dreams. A solution to a problem may be sitting right next to you, but if you neglect to make connections or fail to ask for help from the people you do know, you will miss opportunities, and problems will go unsolved.

One of the most valuable lessons I learned not too long ago was simply just to ask. When faced with a challenge, my old tendency was to answer questions for myself and justify my answers. The problem is that this prevented me from asking for help from people who have more knowledge and experience that could give me the best answer. If we never ask for help, if we neglect to tap into our resources, we will never know how a simple question could have led to an unforeseen solution or opportunity. I would not be slacklining had I not asked someone if I could try their line, and I would not have improved had I not asked to be taught by someone better than me.

I was in a marketing class one day and overheard a kid say to someone how his dad's best friend was the owner of a well-known gym in Fort Collins. I had sat near this kid all semester and had never really talked to him, but I was aware of the gym he was talking about. I thought to myself how great it would be to get connected to that owner. Then that voice in my head told me not to ask. *"You don't know him. Who knows whether or not he is well-connected to the owner? What are you going to say, blah, blah, blah?"* Even though these thoughts flashed through my mind, the next thing I knew, I was asking if the kid could get me connected to the owner. It all worked out, and I now have a connection to a successful gym owner. Even though I was hesitant at first, if I never asked the question, I would have determined my fate.

A lot of students know how important it is to *just ask.* When the semester is coming to an end, and you are a bit concerned about your grades, it can be a great idea to email your teacher to see if they can help you with your final grade. Even though chances are slim, the odds are still better than if you do not ask. I have come across many stories of a student's GPA getting saved because they contacted the teacher and just asked them for help.

Even though the voice in your head sometimes blocks you from asking for help, understand that the voice is there to protect you from failure or embarrassment. But do not buy into that idea of self-protection. Do not hesitate to ask for help. Have the courage to step forward, and you will find most people are more than willing to help, and they often provide killer insights.

LESSON SEVEN

LEARN FROM SUCCESSFUL PEOPLE

"You cannot change your life using the same thinking that got you to where you are now. You have got to give up, to go up."
— *Ryan Miller*

The final lesson in the slackliner's mindset is my favorite. If you can embrace this lesson and make it a part of your life today, it will be like playing the board game Chutes and Ladders. You will be sliding ahead of the competition and into your dreams.

Learn from successful people.

Hands down, this is the most important thing that I have ever learned. You have two choices in life: learn from your mistakes, or learn from the success of other people. Learning from the success of others is the fast track to your dreams.

There are four rock-solid steps to learning from the success of others.
- Find a mentor and coach
- Be coachable
- Clean up your environment
- Develop a mastermind

FIND A MENTOR AND COACH

So many people go through life asking for advice from people who have good intentions but do not have the results to give proper advice. Unless the person you ask has results that you want, do not go around asking just anyone for advice. You would not ask a dentist to teach you heart surgery, nor would you ask a Spanish teacher how to speak German. You certainly would not ask someone to teach you how to slackline if they have never done it before. Finding a mentor or coach who can get you results because they have done it before is a necessity.

The same person could be both mentor and coach, but understand the two different roles. A mentor is someone who has been through the same or similar situation as you and had the results you want. Through their experience, they can give you another perspective and can show you a different way of thinking to help guide you. A coach is someone who can help you think clearly, organize, create action plans and strategies, and develop a system to measure progress. A coach is there when you need help and acts as an accountability partner to keep you moving through the trenches.

When I met my mentors Tony Grebmeier and Michelle Barnes, I realized I knew a lot less than I thought. I had to drop the ego, be teachable and willing to learn. I learned to be resourceful and find the right people to show me the way. Learning from a mentor is one of the best things anyone can do.

BE COACHABLE

In order for things to change in your life, you must first make a change in your life. I have heard this in the past, but never fully understood the true message until I became focused on personal growth. You have to be willing to let go of the things in your life that are not working to make room for new ideas, beliefs, and habits. If you want to let go and make room for something new, you have to be coachable. Being coachable means having a high willingness to learn and a trusting relationship with your coach.

How do you know if you are coachable? Would you be willing to give up something that is important to you so that you can create the time to work on making your dream become a reality? Would you be willing to give up your favorite sport or show, comfort foods, unnecessary extra sleep, frivolous spending, or any other habit or activity for your personal growth? If your answer is yes, you are most likely coachable.

Being coachable can be a challenge because people do not like the feeling of missing out on something they enjoy or having to give up something they love. Most people will resist and refuse to give certain things up for a while to get better results. A great example of this is those people who talk about wanting to be healthy but are not willing to change their eating habits. They would rather be overweight and sick than to start eating healthy foods and exercising. The ones who will not give up to go up will stay down forever.

Working in the health and fitness industry, I make sure that the people I work with are coachable. There is nothing more frustrating than working with someone who wants to improve their life but is resistant to change, or they simply do not want to make minor adjustments in their lifestyle to improve their health.

Since my fitness clients look to me to help them improve their lives, I make sure that I remain very coachable, too, so I can continue to learn and grow. This benefits my clients and me. As a result of my insatiable hunger for personal growth, I become very uncomfortable when I am doing nothing. Only under certain circumstances can I sit and chill and feel like doing nothing is okay. I like to feel like I am productive and making progress toward my dream. There is always room to improve some part of my life. I was told by a previous mentor of mine that getting to the next level in life means less time on pointless media and more time learning and expanding my mind.

When I made a commitment to being coachable, I gave up video games and even TV. I rarely watch movies, and I have found myself to become a big reader. I learned that leaders are readers, and since not all of my mentors are alive or directly accessible, I can learn through the books they have written. I continuously invest my time in personal development and diversify my knowledge through different books, ranging from health and fitness to psychology and sales. Reading these different types of books has added valuable knowledge to me that has increased my credentials and credibility in the fitness industry.

When it comes to learning from successful people, there is nothing more important than being coachable and being willing to take in new information and test it in your own life. Most successful people are coachable. They may not have started out that way, but when they made the internal decision to change their lives and committed to that change, it became easy to follow a mentor and be coachable.

CLEAN UP YOUR ENVIRONMENT

Why do you clean your car, clean your room, and do your laundry? For most people, it is because they want things to be clean and fresh so that they look and feel better about themselves. While these are great habits to develop, did you know that it is far more important to clean up the environment of your day-to-day life?

Maybe you can relate to this. There is nothing like being a broke college student—eating crappy food, trying to pay rent and bills, and barely having enough money left over to party and have a good time. I have been that person multiple times. Looking back over the all the times I was broke, I noticed a pattern. Being a broke college student was a mindset that always kept me broke. Every time I was broke, I had a damn good story to go with it to justify why I was out of money. In fact, pretty much everyone I know who has little or no money has perfected their "broke story." Being broke is just a bunch of excuses stacked together that become a personal story, and if you believe the story, you stay broke. Prosperity is a mindset too. But moving into a prosperity mindset requires you to be coachable, and it starts with cleaning up your environment.

When I first got into personal development, I found myself in a conflict between what I was learning about success and my daily college life. The problem was my environment. My first semester of freshmen year, I got a 1.0 GPA, but damn—I could party! I would have pre-games in my dorm almost every weekend before we went out—especially Thursdays. I was extremely social and made a lot of friends. I still worked out, but I did not have any sense of direction. My environment was people who loved to party, and party a lot. That saying, *"You are who you hang out with,"* is real shit. Fortunately, my best friend, Kyler Graff, one of the other authors in this book, moved back to Colorado. It was through Kyler that I became connected to a mentor who would help give my life meaning and direction.

Through my mentor, I realized the power of having a supportive environment. Having supportive friends who are pushing you to do your best is powerful. It is great to have friends who do not want to see you fail or get hurt. If, however, you have friends whose values and standards conflict with your dreams, cut them off and away from your life. They do this not because they do not believe in you, but because they do not believe in themselves, and they are projecting their self-doubt on you, not wanting to see you get hurt.

When you are committed to building your dreams, you have to have the courage to clean up your environment, even if it means letting go of people who do not fit into your vision of yourself for your future. You do not have to cut them out of your life cold-turkey, but intentionally distance yourself from them until they are no longer a part of your everyday life. It can be painful to do this, but what hurts even more is having the regret of not having pursued your dreams because you allowed the "what if" possibilities to hold you back. *"What if I fail?" "What if they were right, and I was wrong?"* The only "What if" that matters is, *"What if I make this sacrifice and I succeed? How rewarding will that be?"*

I chose to succeed. I had to learn to say no to bad situations. I had to move some people out of my life so that I could grow and make new connections that would allow me to become the person I need to be in order to fulfill my dreams. You can love your friends, but you have to love yourself more so that you can say no to the wrong people and yes to the right people.

Transitioning from a broke mindset into a prosperity mindset is a choice. You have to be willing to clean up your environment by weeding out the negativity. You must get rid of the energy suckers and fill your mind with positivity. Get yourself some supportive friends that lift you up—friends who give you reasons and ways to achieve your dreams.

DEVELOP A MASTERMIND

Have you ever noticed how much easier it is to solve a problem or to be creative when a group of people works together toward a common goal? The old saying that "two heads are better than one" has a lot of truth to it. This idea of putting two or more minds together is called a mastermind. A mastermind is a group of like-minded people who connect for brainstorming, accountability, and to support each other to achieve their goals.

JT, one of my early mentors and business partners, had a mastermind group that I was welcomed into. In this mastermind, we started reading books that would reshape my thinking. The first book we started with was The Law of Success by Napoleon Hill. In this book, Hill introduces the idea of a mastermind and talks about its importance in the process of achieving your dreams. In his words, a mastermind is:

> *"The coordination of knowledge and effort of two or more people who work toward a definite purpose in the spirit of harmony."*

Ever since joining that first mastermind group, I have made it a priority to always be in at least one mastermind, not only because of what I get out of it, but because I have a lot to give. Most people measure their net worth based on their material assets. If you are just starting out in life and have limited assets and you join a mastermind group, it would be number one on your list as the most valuable asset you could ever have. You can start with nothing, and if you have the right people in your life, you can create anything. Seeing how much my life has changed since being part of a mastermind, I must say it is the best thing to have in your portfolio of life.

Napoleon Hill is considered the grand-daddy of personal development. One of the most significant lessons he talks about is finding your definite purpose in life, and to back it with a burning desire. I referred to this earlier as the *end goal*. When I first started reading Hill, I did not have a burning desire for anything, let alone a definite purpose. I just wanted to make a lot of money so I could be free to do as I pleased. After reading that chapter, I spent a few days giving myself a lot of undistracted time alone to think about what I truly wanted in life. The only thing I loved to do was work out and learn about health and fitness. Knowing that life pays for value, I thought out a plan where I could continue to learn and educate myself on fitness and health. Then I would use my knowledge to provide value and information to clients that would help impact their lives for the better.

Had I not been introduced to JT and that mastermind group, who knows if I would have found my chief aim? That is what started a chain of events that led me to write this book.

Looking back to where I was before reading Hill, I now understand that if you do not know what direction you are headed, you will go in circles wasting precious time—the same time that could have been used to pursue your passions.

Humans have a natural desire for achievement and becoming better. When working together in a mastermind, their potential to do anything becomes limitless. If you could join a group of people that helped you fulfill your dreams, what dreams would you want to come true?

Epilogue

*"Leadership is practiced not so much in words
as in attitude and in actions."*
—Harold S. Geneen

When I began to write this book, I had to self-reflect on what I truly believe and what has gotten me to where I am today. I chose the slackliner's analogy because I understand that we are visual learners; we think in pictures. I hope you were able to visualize yourself on that slackline.

In what ways does your life relate to the slackline analogy? Are you just starting out? Are you wobbling? Have you fallen? Wherever you may be on the line, remember the seven key lessons I provided, and use this book as a tool to get you further in life.

The first lesson called for staying focused on the initial step—having an end goal in mind. You have got to know where you are headed and develop an action plan that will make it happen. A plan does not work unless you work it, so follow with action. There are always obstacles along the journey. The key is to overcome those wobbles. Turn any frustration that might appear into motivation, and ditch any excuses you are holding onto. As you are working towards your goal, never take your eyes off the prize. Distractions and challenges will appear, and you may get stressed. Remind yourself to stay calm and not to rush things. A relaxed state of mind will have a much easier time looking at the whole picture and deciding the right move to make.

The second lesson in the slackliner's mindset is to be persistent. People tend to give up or quit when things get hard. Persistence is learning from your mistakes and accepting that it is okay to start over when necessary.

Starting over does not mean you have failed if you are willing to learn from the results of your prior actions. One of the best ways to accept the value of starting over is to measure your progress. Know where you started so you can compare how much you have achieved. Spending a few hours slacklining and not making it across the line may seem like you have not progressed much. However, with all those hours spent practicing and developing the slackliner's mindset, progress has been made. Just find the best way to measure your progress. If you find yourself stuck and what you are doing is not getting you your desired results, do not change your goal; adjust your strategy, instead.

The third key lesson is building your confidence, and it all starts with changing your story. Is the story you are telling yourself adding to your confidence? Your self-belief dictates your actions. However, many people have a habit of focusing on the negative things they do not like about themselves. To help combat this, take inventory of your strengths by asking yourself positive questions. These questions not only set you up to win, but they create a higher belief in yourself and your abilities.

Part of building self-confidence is taking risks, because when a risk works out in your favor, you will be happy and reinforce your confidence. Remember that it is important to celebrate victories, even if they are small. This helps establish a habit of positive self-talk and the right attitude needed for building confidence.

The fourth lesson, to find your balance, is an important factor in developing the slackliner's mindset. The simplest technique to use when you feel stressed or overwhelmed is to breathe and chill. The breath technique brings the body into a relaxed state and supplies the brain with more oxygen, allowing yourself to think more clearly. Taking time for yourself is a necessity if you get caught up in a routine for too long. Changing things up not only keeps life interesting but will keep you sane.

The last part to finding your balance is by listening to feedback from yourself. Our bodies know when we have been running for too long and need a break. Do not disregard this feedback. Instead, listen to it and do something for yourself that changes things up a bit and adds a sense of balance to your life.

Maintaining a positive outlook is the fifth lesson from the slackliner's mindset. Understanding this lesson may seem difficult to those who have a negative outlook, but it is possible to change your perspective. It starts by looking for the win in everything you do. Some wins do not show up right away, which is why it is so crucial to maintain a positive outlook.

Having a can-do attitude is what will drive you through those self-doubting moments. Your belief in yourself must be higher than your self-doubt. A lot of the self-doubt that we create comes from other people's opinions about us that we have listened to and allowed to affect us. Not worrying about other people's opinions is a key factor in determining if you will be able to maintain a positive outlook or not.

Another key lesson in the slackliner's mindset is living in the present moment. We all look for shortcuts in life, but we must follow the process of taking one step at a time. Being present is crucial to knowing when the right moment has arrived to take the next step. Living in the moment means not dwelling on the problems that are not directly affecting you right now. Unless there is something critical and urgent that you must address, most of your problems are in the past or future and are not affecting you in the current moment unless you bring the problem with you and start talking about it and making it real. Use the urgent or important technique to determine when something is worth receiving your time and attention.

Learning how to switch your attention from past and future thinking to the present moment comes from a change in perspective. This ability re-focus your attention to the here-and-now can be tough at first because most people habitually live in the past and future, but it will become easier with more practice.

Lastly, remember the importance of *asking*. You do not have to do everything alone. People are willing and wanting to help. But they cannot help if they do not know you need it.

***

Now that you have read my first book, I hope you were able to take some value away from what I have written and that it helps you find success. The most important thing is to act on any new and fresh ideas that you have in your mind before the initial motivation starts to dwindle.

Be true to yourself and find what you want in life, and then go do it. It is better to take risks now and try new things than to stagnate and become old and have to make changes later in your life after developing years of bad habits, self-limiting beliefs, and deep-rooted, destructive patterns.

If you have beliefs that you need to change and overcome, know that it is possible. Follow the lessons provided in this book, and you can make the change with some consistency and hanging out with the right people. Once that consistency becomes a habit, you will live each day to its fullest.

Share what you have learned from this book with your peers. There are so many people out there struggling who need help or need some mental and emotional connection to feel they are not alone.

Our generation, those of us in our late teens and 20s, need this book more than anyone else. We are at a pivotal point in history where never before have we had such easy access to information and knowledge. The use of technology has created opportunity where it did not exist before. At the same time, this technology and media are keeping our minds occupied and distracted from the real problems of the world, and diverting our attention from our true potential.

Our generation is inheriting a lot of social and environmental problems. We are going to have to take care of our planet, our parents, and our children. But let's not forget the importance of taking care of ourselves first, by developing a healthy mindset, so that we have the strength to take care of each other.

Enjoyed this book?
Share the love...
Tweet, post, Insta...
#ThinkGenWhy
Facebook.com/ThinkGenWhy

Review on Amazon. Go to:
www.ThinkGenWhyBook.com

Acknowledgements

I want to give a special thanks to those people who have left an impact on my life, giving me life experiences and helping me get to where I am today.

Mom: There is so much to thank and recognize you for that it would take another book. Thank you for raising me into the respectful, independent, confident man I am today. Your efforts and love have not gone unnoticed. I love you.

Sarah & Kevin Frank: Thank you for always being there to support me in my endeavors. You helped make this book a reality for me. Love you guys.

Martha Miller (Grandma): Thank you for all you and Grandpa have done for our family and for me. You have made my college experience possible, and I cannot thank you enough.

Matt Wood, Kyler Graff, Ethan Jones, Eric Wright, Jesse Wright: Special thanks to the authors of this book. We started with an idea. Thank you for all your efforts making that idea come to life.

David Strauss: Special thanks for believing enough in us that we developed our own beliefs within ourselves. Thank you for keeping our group intact and pushing us to be our best. We could not have done it without you!

To all my friends who I have been able to build relationships and experience life with, may we each continue to live our own journey and stay connected through this lifespan. You have all taught me valuable lessons and I am grateful for all of you.

Thanks to: Amber Grebmeier, Anastasia Monsell, Andrew Peterson, Brian Froechtenigt, Brittany Lucas, Christian Dean, Dominic Alarid, Evan Jenkins, Jake Walker, Jon Friedman, Josh Marchena, Kyle Cooper, Lauren Workman, and Tony Grebmeier.

Thanks to all my friends from MVHS, Cheer, Parm Farm, Aspen Heights, LIT Snap, Networking Events, and Fort Collins.

...and anyone else who has impacted my life!

BOOK FIVE

THE FAITH CODE

FIVE INSIGHTS TO SHAPE YOUR LIFE

• ETHAN JONES •

Prologue

"A healthy mind observes and questions itself. This is the path to inner peace and happiness. Don't believe everything you think."
— Vironika Tugaleva

Have you ever wondered why some people seem very happy and have a lot of self-confidence and direction, while other people struggle with accepting who they are and living with a positive outlook on life? This is extremely prevalent in kids in their teens and 20s, especially within our generation.

Ever since I was a kid, I struggled with my self-image; nothing too heavy, just the fact that I did not always feel like I fit in with everyone else. For me, life was like a glass of water. The glass represents me as a physical person, and the water would represent my personality, including my beliefs, limitations, feelings, fears, emotions, and self-image. I was usually the guy who would see the glass as half-empty. I could not say that I was always optimistic about my life. At times, I felt like I was all alone and no one was there to help me figure out who I truly am, how to find my purpose, or how to become a happy and confident person.

I struggled in high school socially and was uneasy when it came to knowing who my true friends were. I would bounce back-and-forth between friend groups based on my interests. I had no clue what I wanted to do with my life. I had no direction. I was never one of your typical A or B students. I did not learn very much because I learned differently than every other student, yet from day one the school system would always try to tell me what was best for me and how I should learn. Even though I wanted to fit in and be accepted by others, I never wanted to be like everyone else.

Rather, I wanted to do my own thing and find my own solution to the issues that I faced. Even though teachers want their students to succeed, I felt like the system was set up for us to fail if we veer off their predetermined path.

One of my struggles was that I had been taught that a person's success is measured only based on their financial accomplishments, not the contributions they have made to humanity during their lifetime. This idea was etched into my brain from a very young age, causing a fear of whether or not I would be successful. I was using someone else's definition of success instead of my own. The problem with this is that It caused me to fear taking action because I knew how difficult it would be to become a successful person living by these terms. It was like living life and looking at the world from the outside-in, using someone else's rules and standards, instead of the inside-out by creating and using my own rules and standards.

My turning point hit me when I was 18 years old. I had just finished high school and was taking a gap year off. I had done some traveling and spent some time working, but I was not necessarily doing anything constructive with my life. I would sometimes feel down on myself and lonely, imagining the things that could happen next. I was not going in any particular direction, and I knew that. I was thinking negatively; therefore, I remained negative. When I was starting to feel down, my mood did not improve. I imagined the things that a lot of kids would imagine at this stage in my life:

- Worrying about being on my own
- Taking on unmanageable debt
- The pressure of getting a job to support a future family
- Having to grow up instantly
- Not having a clear direction for my life

Instead of using my imagination to create and plan my future, I was using it to focus on all the negative things. I did not realize at the time that thoughts become things. But then one of my best friends since the age of four asked me to work with him. I went from making five dollars an hour, plus tips, to making $19 per hour. I was so stoked! It was a pretty cool gig, and I got the chance to meet some exceptional guys that would leave an impact on my life forever.

I started working at a private Amazon.com seller's distribution warehouse with positive-minded, uplifting people who challenged me to think in a new way that I had never thought before. Not only did they show me the ropes, they also showed me behind-the-scenes what it takes to run a successful business, as well as how to invest properly. It was there that

PROLOGUE

I realized I was too focused on my emotions and things that did not really matter, and those emotions were distracting me from my true purpose. That experience in the warehouse is what helped me to turn my life around.

It is amazing how much power the mind has, and I did not realize it until one of the guys was talking with me about a quote that I had heard at some point earlier in my life, but now it had a whole new meaning that helped to shift my paradigm of thinking.

"What you think, you become. What you feel, you attract. What you imagine, you create." — *Unknown*

Even though I had heard it before, this time someone was explaining the meaning behind it. I am responsible for my life based on what I think, feel, and imagine. Something clicked. Have you ever had that moment where something so simple just fits into place, almost like a new understanding of a specific topic, an *aha* moment? That was when my mindset shifted from one of a dependent, insecure, and unmotivated individual, to that of an independent, confident, and inspired young man.

I am not saying that one quote changed me completely, but it caused me to look closely at my life and begin to make big changes in how I was thinking and the people I surrounded myself with. I started realizing that the water in my glass—my personality, beliefs, limitations, feelings, fears, emotions, and self-image—was reflecting who I was on the inside, and it would only change if I changed my thought process.

Once I realized that I am in control of my happiness, self-confidence, and the direction of life, I no longer saw my glass as half-empty. Instead, I saw a new reflection within myself that is based on five lessons that have and will continue to shape my life.

- Be open to making changes
- Commit to personal growth
- Be a coachable person
- Develop a healthy mindset
- Take responsibility for your outcome

As I began to apply these lessons into my life, my glass began to overflow with a renewed sense of hope for making a difference in the world and greater faith in my future. Through this fresh perspective, I developed a new sense of purpose and direction for my life, which I talk about in this book. As I share my perspective on these five points, it is my hope that they help you as much as they have helped me.

Lesson One

Be Open to Making Changes

"Change is inevitable. Growth is optional."
— *John C. Maxwell*

It is no mystery that life is all about change. It happens throughout our lives. We come into this world, completely dependent on our parents, but we change over time. We adapt and eventually become independent. At times, the changes can be highly unpredictable. Other times, they can flow with ease. No two moments are the same. The will to change cannot be forced upon us; there is an internal chain of reactions that must first take place.

How do you know if you are ready to change? It is pretty easy to tell most of the time, because some part of you will feel uncertain, or it could be the fact that the things you're currently doing just aren't working out. It could be that uneasy feeling in your gut which is signaling that you are ready to try something new. Beyond the ordinary need for variety in life, sometimes you have no choice. Life can be harsh, and often we must become motivated by desperation rather than inspiration. Other times you can be inspired by a new idea or fresh view of life that triggers the desire to try something new. Regardless of your motivation—be it inspiration or desperation—nothing happens until you become open to new possibilities for your life. For me, there are six steps to making changes.

1) Be honest with yourself
2) Identify your obstacles
3) Take inventory
4) Set yourself up to win
5) Get the right resources
6) Make a plan, and take action

BE HONEST WITH YOURSELF

The first step to being open to change is to be honest with yourself about where you are now. You do not have to like the way things are, but you have to be brutally honest with yourself about everything that is going on in your life right now. You have to know your starting point before you can choose a new direction.

In order to figure out where you are right now—your starting point—you need to spend time answering one simple question that will help you to become more self-aware. Write this question down.

What is working in my life, and what is not working?

These could be habits or relationships, or anything else that either helps you move forward or holds you back. Once you've identified what is and is not working, the next step to making changes is to decide where you want to go. What changes do you want to make in your life?

- Do you want a new career?
- Are you ready to improve your health and fitness?
- Do you want to clear out toxic people from your life?
- Do you have any bad habits you want to eliminate?
- Are you ready for a new relationship?
- What can you do that will make you happy?
- Do you want to improve your finances?
- Are you ready to have a family?
- Do you want to travel more?

A lot of people have a hard time deciding what they want due to how much is going on in their life at the moment. They may feel overwhelmed with family responsibilities, stress from work, financial pressure, challenges with their health, or any other situation that tugs at their time, energy, or emotions. When you become aware of these distractions, it gives you the opportunity to realize where you are focusing most of your time and energy so that you can shift your focus to a much more constructive, useful purpose.

A good way to clear your head so that you can reset your focus is to find a way to mentally and emotionally escape from your daily routine. Go on a hike or walk. Go somewhere that you can get away from the stress of your daily lifestyle and listen to your thoughts without any outside influences. When was the last time you had a conversation with yourself without distractions?

IDENTIFY YOUR OBSTACLES

Once you have become clear about what you want, and you see these changes as the focal points in your life, you then have to identify the obstacles that will hold you back from making progress.

It is no secret that there are many obstacles that you will come across throughout your life. Some of those obstacles are internal, and others are external. Internal obstacles are your thoughts, fears, and beliefs. External obstacles are people and situations.

Your biggest obstacles are your fears, which are rooted in your thoughts and beliefs. You are born with only two fears—the fear of falling and the fear of loud noises. All other fears are either made up in your mind or learned during your childhood from people and your environment, and they affect your everyday life. All fears have the same result: they stop you from taking action. That is, until you learn how to use fear as fuel for motivation.

Your obstacles are not there to prevent you from succeeding. They are there to guide you. Once you identify your obstacles, it then becomes very clear that they are part of the route to success.

Steve Jobs did not become successful overnight. He had many hills and valleys to navigate before he finally created the perfect product. The same goes for Barry Sanders, the Detroit Lions running back. Before he entered the NFL, he was probably told that he was not big enough, strong enough, or fast enough, but he pursued his dream anyway. He navigated the obstacles. He hit the weight room and trained day-in and day-out to become the best he could be. He had many obstacles, which led to his success.

Your obstacles define you and become a part of you. You can measure your willpower based upon the size of the obstacle that stops you.

TAKE INVENTORY

Being open to making changes requires you to take a self-inventory of your thoughts, beliefs, strengths, and weaknesses. When taking your inventory, you want to write everything down so that your list is a visual representation of where you are at in your life. This list will make it easier to think about how each thought, belief, strength, or weakness affects your life. You want to do this so that you become aware of how they form into fears and where they may be causing roadblocks in your life.

Learn to take responsibility as quickly as possible for anything that holds you back so that you can redirect your attention in a more productive direction. For some people, this can be easy because they want to make changes in their life so badly that they are willing to let go of anything that does not serve their higher good. At the same time, taking inventory of yourself can be challenging for a lot of people because you have to admit your faults and weaknesses.

SET YOURSELF UP TO WIN

When facing your fears with the intention of overcoming them, you have to set yourself up to win by stacking small wins so that you can build your self-confidence. For example, if you want to read one book per month but have not read a book in ages, start with a smaller goal of reading one page per day for 30 days until you develop a new reading habit, and then increase your goal. If you want to get fit but have not worked out in a while, start with an easy 30-day workout schedule that you know you can keep, and build your habit and confidence from there. If you want to lose weight, when you go grocery shopping, avoid the snack aisles. You can also start hanging out with people who have successfully lost weight so that their enthusiasm rubs off on you.

When you cross something off your daily schedule or accomplish a goal you set for yourself, you feel good. When you continuously get things done, you feel great. When you set yourself up every day with ways to win, it increases your confidence in your ability to achieve more. This will lead to building healthy habits in all aspects of your life and will eventually begin to flow into other people's lives and create an impact on them as well.

Your motivation alone is not always enough to set yourself up to win, because motivation only lasts so long. Sometimes it takes proving to yourself that you have what it takes to get yourself to the next level. You cannot look at where you are at now and allow your current results to determine the results of your future. You are always capable of the next, higher level of achievement.

Setting yourself up to win starts with planning ahead and planning smart. Plan your tomorrow today so that you do not become stressed and overwhelmed and live with a reaction-based mindset.

GET THE RIGHT RESOURCES

When you make changes in your life, it creates a lot of uncertainty, which can add discomfort to your current situation. The easiest way to ease the discomfort is to find the right resources to release the pressure. The best resources are always people who have your back and can give you solid advice.

You do not want to be taking relationship advice from the guy who has never had a sustained relationship. But you would want to talk to the guy who has had thriving relationships. You would not want to listen to the guy who sits on his couch all day watching TV, telling you how he can make money. You want to be talking to the guy who reads every day and is actually making six figures per year.

The reality of change is that no matter how smart you are, you will face challenges. Few people realize that it is necessary for you to go through challenges to get you to where you want to go. If you were just given everything in the beginning on a silver platter, you would not learn about dedication and hard work. You also would not go through the struggles that define the low points, and most importantly, the lows that define the highs in life. That is why it is important to choose your resources wisely, because they can help you navigate through the challenges.

If you truly want a change, you must be open to it. If you are open, then you will be amazed as to what may come into your life. Successful people realize that change always happens for a reason. They also know how to find the right resources to make sure the change works out in their own best interest.

MAKE A PLAN, AND TAKE ACTION

When you reach the point of being open to making changes, nothing happens until you make a plan, and take action. Once you have decided on the direction you want to go, you have to set specific and realistic goals to get there and make a commitment to the action steps so that you can begin making the change you want.

Moving a plan into action feels great, but nothing ever gets done the first time without taking that first step in the right direction. The first step would be tapping into your inner-motivation. This means finding out what gets you going and excited to wake up at the beginning of the day. Inner-motivation is the driving force behind action.

One thing I recommend that you do every single day when you wake up is to write out your goals for the future, and make sure to include what

you are thankful for every day as well.
- What are your goals one, three, and six months out?
- Where do you want to be one year, two years, five years, and 10 years from now?
- What steps will you take to make sure you accomplish those goals?
- What are you most thankful for?

Writing out your goals every day strengthens the neuro-connections in your brain, which increases your focus and belief in your goals. Once you know what you want to accomplish, the next step is to develop a strong action plan so that you stay motivated to crush those goals. A person without goals or an action plan is just wandering through life, and there is a high chance they will not achieve what they want to within their lifetime.

When making your action plan, you have to determine exactly what it will take to reach your goals, and then go at it with 10 times the effort. Create small goals at first to set yourself up to win. This builds your confidence and digs in and advances you toward your goals.

Your goals only work as hard as you do. You can sit around talking about them, but until you actually start to actively engage in what you are doing, you will see no results.

If you are trying to achieve something completely new to you, you will have to exercise your ability to think a bit differently. Be open-minded to new possibilities and new ways of looking at your situation. Do not be afraid of change. If you cannot let go of what is not currently working in your life, then how can you expect to create a new future for yourself?

LESSON TWO

COMMIT TO PERSONAL GROWTH

*"Those who improve with age embrace the power of
personal growth and personal achievement and begin to replace
youth with wisdom, innocence with understanding,
and lack of purpose with self-actualization."*
—Bo Bennett

An acorn cannot become an oak tree without growth and change. People are no different. If you want something new, you have to be willing to become something new, and that takes action with a definite plan in mind.

A lot of people want to move their life in a different direction but are not willing to commit to hurdling the obstacles currently in their way that are necessary to improve their beliefs and thoughts. They are afraid to try something new, and so they "hope" for new results but never do anything different to get those new results. It is as if they want the whole world to change so that they do not have to. If you want your life to improve, you must be willing to make the little changes in the beginning, which will result in the big change in the end.

When you have a vision of who you want to become or what you want your life to be like, in order to make that vision a reality you must first acknowledge and accept your current self so that you have an honest assessment of where you are. Visions come and go, as do people. Once you have made an honest assessment of yourself, you need to develop your vision, and every day ask yourself, *"If today was my last day here, would I want to do what I'm doing today?"* You really must evaluate this, and if you decide that you are not happy with your answer, then it's time to change things up a little bit. Making changes will spark the fire of your desire to become your ideal self.

If you want to uncover your potential and take yourself from being an acorn to an oak, these four simple steps will put you on a trajectory of growth.

- Find coaches and mentors
- Establish healthy habits
- Keep your commitments
- Develop a support team

FIND COACHES AND MENTORS

For every goal or accolade I have achieved in my life, I could trace it back to a coach and mentor that helped me achieve it. One lesson that was taught to me during my freshman year at lacrosse practice stands out as an example of the value of having a coach or mentor. I would always hear my coach yelling:

"Hard work beats talent when talent doesn't work hard."

One day after practice, I walked up to my coach and asked how I can get better. What he told me took me by surprise. He said, *"If you outwork everyone else on the field, you will be the best."* I will never forget this, because it taught me the power of dedication. He also told me that he would rather have a player on the field who is working his tail off than the player who has talent and is not working for it. I then realized that the thing I needed to do most to improve my skill level was to make sure I was working harder than anyone else on the team. If I just work harder than anyone else, I would develop a work ethic that is always raising my threshold of achievement.

After learning and applying my coach's lesson into my day-to-day life, things began to change. That one lesson made me realize that whatever I want to accomplish in life, I can shorten the learning curve by getting a coach and mentor who is going to kick-start me onto the right path so that I can achieve my desired accomplishment.

LESSON TWO: COMMIT TO PERSONAL GROWTH

We all have dreams and goals, but they stay as a dream or goal until we make a move and take action. It is true that the hardest part of accomplishing anything is getting started, but that is only half-correct. The toughest part is getting started in the right direction, and that is much easier with a coach and mentor.

When you have a mentor, you are substantially increasing your likelihood of success because you are learning from someone who has already arrived at where you want to be, and you get to see the path without all the mistakes that they have made. Through attentive listening, you get to take notes on exactly what it takes to get there and the sacrifices that need to be made. Finding mentors will also build your confidence in the sense that they can give you advice that most other people cannot, so that you can make good decisions. As long as you pay attention and do what you are told, you will build your confidence and pick up your success much faster than you would learn on your own.

A coach allows you to fine-tune and apply the insights of a mentor. They provide a more action-oriented and structured relationship that helps you to identify your strengths and weaknesses, become clear about your needs and goals, and develop action plans. Emphasis is on the assessment and monitoring of results, and cleaning up your thoughts and limiting beliefs. A coach does not necessarily have the results that you want, but they can help you develop the strategic thinking to find the right resources and take the best actions to get those results.

The time will never come when you know it all, and you do not need any more coaching or mentoring. There is always the next level of success to achieve, and the need to learn and grow as a person never goes away. When you have a coach and mentor, they will always be looking out for you no matter what the situation is. It can also open doors for you. They probably have a lot of quality contacts and may know someone, or even themselves, who may be looking to hire someone. What kind of person do you think they are looking for? Would it be a stranger with a résumé, or someone they know and trust on a personal level?

Any good and smart coach or mentor is not going to take time out of their busy life to invest in you for free, but you do not always have to pay for your mentor financially. In some situations, you can offer them some equal or greater value in return for their time and insight. Either way, make sure you listen to them and show them respect, because after all, they are there to help you. Be sure to show appreciation to someone for investing their time to help you, and be thankful for the direction they are giving you because it is invaluable.

ESTABLISH HEALTHY HABITS

If you want to plant a thriving garden, you cannot water it only when you feel like it. Plants do not blossom based on emotional choices. They require consistent watering and care to thrive. The same is true with people. If you want to commit yourself toward your own personal growth and create a new life for yourself, you have to establish consistent, healthy habits.

It is probably safe to say that for most people, creating good habits is not their strength. But if you want to commit to personal growth, it is very important to establish a pattern of healthy habits so that you can prepare yourself to reach your goals.

When you begin to establish new habits, you must be patient, because changing habits rarely occurs overnight. Success is not an overnight destination. When you forge a new path for yourself, at first, you still have the lingering effects of your old choices and outdated behavior patterns that will distract you and pull you from your new habits. You have to be strong enough to stop old patterns from sabotaging the new direction you are taking your life. It is also important to shift your focus from short-term to long-term so that you can see the changes unfold in your life as you move forward. Every decision has a consequence, positive or negative.

Old habits are very hard to break because they are stitched into your brain and personality. Once you make the commitment to building new habits and acting on them daily, your brain begins to build new neuropathways to reinforce your new patterns. This means you are actually rewiring your brain to think and act differently. Old habits and beliefs are never *unwired*. As your new habits become a stronger and more dominant force in your daily life, they will override your old patterns. Your newly rewired brain will then allow your new habits to create your healthy-habits life.

Here are a few steps you can follow to establish your new, healthy habits.
- Write a list of all the good and harmful habits in your life.
- Identify the benefits of all your good habits.
- List the consequences of your harmful habits.

Once you have your list, ask yourself these three questions:
- How can you create more beneficial habits for your life?
- What can you do to replace destructive habits with good ones?
- What resistance or obstacles do you need to overcome to do this?

Creating new healthy habits comes down to creating a game plan to change your beliefs and attitudes, and hence, your brain's chemistry so that your negative habits and destructive patterns are no longer a part of your everyday routine. This may include not watching as much TV, or replacing TV with reading. You may choose to spend less time with people who have a bad influence on you, and more time with quality people. Whatever you choose, it is completely necessary to isolate your bad habits and work toward replacing them with healthy habits that lead to greater happiness and productivity.

One of the best habits to create is planning your tomorrow the day before. Early planning improves time management and makes it easy to measure your progress. For most people, if you were to write out your plan for the next day the night before, you would typically save an average of three hours per day. That is three more hours to be productive and take action towards reaching your goals.

Establishing healthy habits is a big step in personal growth. They go hand-in-hand because you cannot make changes to your life if you are locked into the same habits and mindset that got you there. Once your new habits are established and become a regular part of your day, you will find your life quickly improving.

KEEP YOUR COMMITMENTS

The benefits of establishing healthy habits are only as valuable as your ability to make commitments to your decisions. As soon as you make a commitment to yourself or someone else, it is important to know that commitments don't keep themselves. Ironically, you have to be committed to keeping that commitment.

If you make commitments to other people and you cannot hold up your end, and it happens over and over, you are developing a belief that it is okay to break commitments. Once you make it a habit of breaking commitments, eventually you will lose your sense of urgency to keeping commitments and you no longer take yourself seriously. You will slip into a mindset of making excuses and justifying your shortcomings and failures.

Obviously, there are times when life just gets in the way, and you cannot make good on your promises to other people. The way you deal with that with integrity is to communicate in advance that you cannot keep your promise, and you come up with a new agreement. This is much better than blowing someone off and giving excuses afterward. The easiest way to keep commitments to yourself is to plan your days in advance so that you do not become overwhelmed with responsibilities, and then fall into a pattern of rationalizing and not doing things.

How many times have you told yourself that you are going to start working out, lose that body fat, and get in shape? You *decide* to go to the gym multiple times a week, you get started in your new routine, and then one day you do not feel like doing your exercises, so you skip going to the gym. Then, another day comes up the next week, and you make an excuse: *"Oh, I'm just too busy,"* or, *"I don't feel like working out today."*

On those days that you decided to skip, you are weakening your mind and willpower and giving strength to the belief that it is "okay" to skip these days. In reality, those few days of skipping become the reason why you give up so quickly. One of the secrets to keeping commitments is developing a support team.

DEVELOP A SUPPORT TEAM

How good does it feel when you first meet up with a friend or family member, and the first thing they do is give a genuine compliment to you and ask how you are doing? It is a fantastic feeling. Now, how good does it feel when you are with people who always find the negatives in life and provide no moral support for you? It does not make you feel too good about yourself. It's very easy to tell which relationships in your life suck the energy out and which ones make you feel energized.

Along with finding coaches and mentors, and creating healthy habits, you need to gather up a support group that wants you to succeed and will help you to build upon your successes. These people have your best interest held genuinely, and they care about how you are doing. Developing a strong team of people who are there for you and genuinely support you and push you to become the best person you can be is a key ingredient to your personal growth. Gathering your team together is the beginning. Keeping them together is progress. Working together is success.

"Nothing great was ever accomplished alone."

When I look at my life now compared to only a couple of years ago, my greatest progress and biggest influence comes from having a support group. The people in my life who truly know me know that my deepest desire in life is to make this world a better place and just spread positivity. I am lucky to have found so many amazing people who believe in me and help me to believe in myself and my vision for our generation.

Your support team is only as good as your commitment to personal growth. No one can make the changes for you. If you are truly committed to making your life the best it can be, then, by all means, develop a support team, and make sure it only consists of people who care to see you grow, want to excel with you, and are excited to see you succeed. Forget those who laugh at your efforts or try to drag you down because they do not believe in themselves. These people have no place in your life as they will only serve as a distraction.

LESSON THREE

BE COACHABLE

*"Coachable people seek out those who speak truth to them,
even if it is a painful truth because it protects them
and it makes them a better person and leader."*
— Gary Rohrmayer

Have you ever noticed that some people have a need to always be right? I know how frustrating it can be, because I used to be that person. Ever since I was growing up, I always had this sense of pride where I always needed to be right. I mean, someone could literally prove me wrong, and I would still try to find a way to make myself feel right. Part of me believes that it is our nature to want to be right. It is a form of self-protection. No one wants to be wrong, and we have a hard time owning up to it. But a lot of the time our need to be right is because we want to be accepted by others, and if we are wrong about something it may make us seem unintelligent or unlikeable.

It is also important to understand not every action needs a reaction. If you are wrong and you know it, just own it. There is no need to react in a way that will cause embarrassment or make you look insecure. Stay humble and admit you were wrong, and it will do more for you than if you are trying to justify that you are somewhat right.

The biggest hazard from the need to be right is that it also means that you are close-minded and cannot learn anything new. When I first started hanging out with a winning crowd, my need to be right virtually disappeared. Everyone who I was hanging out with was committed to learning and improving themselves, and I wanted to get in on the fun. I went from being close-minded to being coachable.

I cannot think of a more valuable trait than being coachable and having a high willingness to learn. Being a coachable person is like kicking down all the roadblocks to your potential. For me, being coachable includes four personality traits that allow you to learn and apply new ideas.

- Be humble and open-minded
- Be action-oriented
- Be willing to try new things
- Live with active faith

With these four traits in mind I have learned that instead of always being right, it is better to take an interest in what others are saying and consider them more important than yourself. Be quick to listen and slow to share your own opinions, and you will be amazed how much more people will respect you.

To put things in perspective, how can you expect to truly make a difference in someone else's life without first being a coachable person to yourself. If you are working with a coach or mentor and you are not a shapeable person, the only thing that will grow is frustration.

Be Humble and Open-Minded

Being humble is one of the most important makings of being coachable. People who are humble do not boast of their success, because they realize that success is a team sport. Some of the most successful people are the noticeably humble, because they understand that the things they want to learn cannot be learned on their own. There are some things that need to be completed with the help of others. The quarterback cannot advance the ball without the help of his wide receivers and running back. A ship's captain cannot navigate the vessel without the crew. If you want to succeed in life, you have to humble yourself and realize that your wins will come from the help of others.

A big part of being humble is being open-minded. When you are humble, you are open to new ideas and new ways of thinking. You are willing to make yourself vulnerable, even if it is uncomfortable, so that you set yourself up to win. People who are coachable are enthusiastically humble and open-minded, because they know the value of learning from other people's experiences.

There is also a dependability factor that comes with humility. When people see that you have the right attitude and are not full of yourself, you appear to be more reliable, which means they can count on you when they need help.

Be Action-Oriented

Being coachable means being action-oriented. You must be willing to get up off your ass and put in the required work. When you are taking direction from your mentor or coach, or are working with your support team, none of them will accept any excuses. Being action-oriented requires humility and open-mindedness, because sometimes you will be doing things outside of your comfort zone.

"Take an action, not make a reaction."

There are productive actions and counter-productive reactions. If there is an issue that you are facing and you cannot seem to get past it, do not just react by sitting there and complaining. Instead, take action, analyze the issue, and come to a solution. Do not be that person who is always blaming outside circumstances for their misfortunes. People who are coachable do not look outside themselves or justify their shortcomings. They look at their own behaviors and find ways to self-correct.

Be Willing to Try New Things

For some people, the hardest part of being coachable is being willing to try new things. Every time you try something new or different, you risk the possibility of failure, and for a lot of people, that is one of their biggest fears. It is okay to be afraid, but do not let it stop you, because failures build the foundation for success. When you fail at something, if you do not allow yourself to become consumed by it, you can gain valuable insight into what does and does not work.

No one likes to fail, but failure can guide you to develop self-correcting habits. When you figure out what went wrong, you gain the mental sharpness to not repeat those same mistakes. Even though the failures can be painful, being willing to try new things makes life much more fun and interesting.

If you want to try something new, either for the fun of it or because you have to make a change in your life, coming at it with a *can-do* attitude and an open mind will increase your chances of success and expand your knowledge and abilities. Plus, with a can-do attitude, you are more willing to persevere through unknown challenges and keep committed to your outcome.

Live With Active Faith

People who are willing to try new things live with active faith. They have the courage to make the decision to start something new, even if they do not know exactly how they are going to accomplish what they set out to do. It is one thing to believe in something, but it is another thing to take action based on that belief.

Being coachable means that when you get started with something new, you are willing to test your faith in yourself by taking action. You are willing to take those first steps because what you are doing is in sync with your values and beliefs, and you have the confidence that you can do it.

People who are coachable, when faced with the need or desire to change, make decisions with active faith based on their confidence in their ability to get new results. For some people, as with me, their faith in themselves is an extension of their faith and belief in God.

Active faith can be demonstrated in both short- and long-term goals.

Short-term active faith is when you get caught up. At the moment, maybe things just aren't going the way you want right now, and at first, you get frustrated, but then you get over yourself and take responsibility for the situation. You begin by building up the courage to make changes in your life despite the fact that it may be difficult or painful. You get out of a bad relationship or quit a job that makes you feel lousy or anything that will allow you to quickly get out of pain, anger, or frustration.

Long-term active faith would be living in a way that you think about the effects of your decisions before committing to them, and are willing to make long-term decisions because of your strong belief in yourself, and for some people, also their belief in God. When you live with active faith, it is because you understand that you have control over your outcome since you are in control of your choices.

This idea of active faith is like a code of honor for how you will make decisions. I call it the *Faith Code.* It is a set of agreements that you make with yourself about how you live your life. My Faith Code is that I put God first in my life, and I do my best to help others and to be a bright light for those who are in emotionally dark places.

In my Faith Code, I have agreed to look for the good in every situation and to focus on being of service to others, rather than always focusing on my own needs. I agree to be a good listener and to make decisions with their long-term impact in mind.

If you want to develop your own Faith Code, ask yourself how you are going to react to life in any given situation.

Are you going to let your downfalls hold you back or launch you forward? Are you going to make decisions based on only what is good for you, or are you going to be considerate of others, as well? When faced with surprise challenges, are you going to make short-term active-faith decisions, or be indecisive and squander your chance to learn and grow?

Living with active faith is a personal choice. Either you want to learn from difficulties and become a better person, or are willing to get lost in the drama of your frustrations and failures. You get to decide.

LESSON FOUR

DEVELOP A HEALTHY MINDSET

"Before you diagnose yourself with depression or low self-esteem, first make sure that you are not, in fact, just surrounding yourself with assholes."
—Unknown

Have you ever been in a position where you are looking to advance towards something? This could be a job promotion, moving into a nicer house, or setting up ideas and plans to reach a milestone in your life, but you do not know how to get there, and you get stuck in a helpless feeling. I know I have. The sad thing is, a lot of people go through their entire life stuck in that helpless feeling no matter what they want to do. They do not know how to make a decision and take action. The way to overcome feeling perpetually stuck is to develop a healthy mindset. There are four building blocks to developing a healthy mindset which have worked very well in my life.

- Eliminate negative influences
- Think in terms of happiness
- Read and listen to empowering books
- Find a mastermind group

ELIMINATE NEGATIVE INFLUENCES

The first and most important building block to developing a healthy mindset is to accept the fact that you have obstructions in your life that could be holding you back from reaching your true potential.

Two of the most common obstructions include:
- Destructive self-talk
- Toxic relationships

DESTRUCTIVE SELF-TALK

It is easy to blame hesitations and failures on other people and outside events, but in reality, the biggest roadblock to achievement is destructive self-talk.

Our inner-conversation is what makes us or breaks us. People who struggle with achievement typically talk to themselves in a destructive manner.

- What's wrong with me?
- Why can't I figure this stuff out?
- How come I always screw up?
- Why am I such a loser?
- How come no one likes me?

The consequences of negative self-talk are far reaching. You have to be careful about what you say to yourself because you are also listening and agreeing to your voice. Your inner-conversation can lower your self-confidence, crush your self-esteem, and diminish your happiness. Consider these three points if you want to clean up your destructive self talk.

1) Identify Your Triggers: What makes you sink into a self-doubting or shameful spiral? It can be specific words, people, or situations. Once you identify these, come up with a strategy to challenge them and replace them with an empowering response.

2) Eliminate Absolutes: Most negative self-talk includes words like, "never" or "always." These self-imprisoning words prevent you from learning, because when you identify with these absolutes you have to live with them as part of your identity, and they prevent you from seeing the positive side.

3) Come up with an empowering alternative: This is where having a coach or mentor comes in handy. Once you have identified your triggers and absolutes, you want to come up with a strategy to replace

them with empowering alternatives that lead to you feeling stronger and more confident about yourself. For example, if you do not like the way your body looks, instead of saying, *"I will never be fit,"* you want to reassure yourself that it is only a temporary situation and reaffirm yourself that you can change your situation.

When you clean up your self-talk, you are making steps to cleaning up your relationship with yourself. The next big step is to clear out toxic relationships from your life.

TOXIC RELATIONSHIPS

Would you drink water from a pipe that is pouring sewage into a river? Of course not. It could make you sick or kill you. If you think of your mind as that river, would you want to let negative people pour their toxic ideas and beliefs into your mind? Absolutely not, but people do it all the time.

One of the most valuable gifts you can give to yourself is to eliminate the negative relationships from your life that are holding you back mentally, physically, and emotionally. When I first started getting rid of the people who were making my life intolerable, it was like taking blinders off of my self-confidence; everything changed for the better.

Take a moment to identify all the negative individuals in your life. Then take a moment and picture how much different the outcome of your day would be without their negative influence.

How can you tell if someone does not belong in your life?
- Do they cause you to doubt yourself?
- Do they drain the energy from you?
- Do they waste your time or take your time for granted?
- Do they display envy or jealousy towards you?
- Do they make you feel bad?
- Are they always emphasizing the bad, even in good situations?
- Do you have to bend over backward to accommodate them or make them happy?

If you answered yes to any of these, then do whatever it takes to get these people out ASAP. The only purpose they serve in your life is to suck the energy out of you and alter your mood. They may not do it intentionally. They may not be bad people. They likely have unresolved issues in their life, but that does not mean they belong in your life.

You may not be able to get all of the energy suckers out of your life. Some may be family or other people who are an inescapable part of your everyday life. For those people who you cannot fully exclude, it is important to establish boundaries with them to limit the influence of their negativity in your life.

When you set a boundary, you are taking responsibility for the people you allow into your environment. You are also letting the other people know that their involvement in your life is conditional upon pre-set agreements. You do this not because you do not like them, but because you love yourself more, and are willing to set these new standards of what is and is not acceptable in your life.

Once you establish a boundary with someone, you have cleared up mental and emotional space to allow more goodness into your life. Now, instead of being affected by the energy suckers, you can positively influence them through the example of your new, positive mindset. You combat the negative with some positive.

When you learn how to counter negativity with a positive attitude, it helps to diffuse a negative atmosphere and makes others feel happier about themselves and their life.

Once you have cleared out the obstructions of negative self-talk and toxic relationships, you will be changed in a way that you will no longer be overwhelmed by negative people or thoughts. Instead, you will develop strong relationships with people who will challenge you to try new things and will push you to be the best you can be. Healthy habits will begin to consume your life, causing you to be more enthusiastic about your future. Happiness will radiate throughout every interaction in your life, and you will start to attract like-minded people with the same values as yourself. At last, you will be able to learn from the past and move on to new and better ways of living.

THINK IN TERMS OF HAPPINESS

When I graduated high school, I was dead set on the fact that I wanted to fly in the Air Force. In order to do that, I would have to go to flight school for four years and sign a contract for six years. Just having graduated, I did not know if I was ready for another four years of school. I had this lingering feeling that I would be missing out on other opportunities. I went back-and-forth asking my parents and friends what was right.

I did not know what my true path was. I was lost and confused. I quickly realized that sometimes you need some help from those closest to you to help you progress to your next stage in life. One day I asked a good friend of mine what he would think of me if I were to decide to not join the Air Force. What he told me I would never forget. He said to me:

"All that matters in the end is your happiness. If you do not like what you do, then you won't be happy in life. Without happiness, life is bland and boring. Find those people who support you no matter what you do because those are the ones who will be there to see you truly happy and succeed."

What I took from this is that it does not really matter what direction you take your life as long as it contributes to your happiness. Your current mindset and the choices you make either limit or maximize your full potential. Making decisions that develop a healthy, happy mind is the way to succeeding in life.

Everything that you think of or dream about reflects the mindset you are in at that time. If you want to think in terms of happiness, it is helpful to understand that your brain works in a cycle:

- Beliefs determine actions
- Actions feed results
- Results reinforce beliefs
- Beliefs determine mindset
- Mindset unleashes potential

That being said, there is no doubt that your beliefs control your mindset. Your beliefs do have power and can help you accomplish your goals. The trick to enabling your beliefs to help you succeed is to set up daily routines that reinforce your beliefs, so that you get done what you need to do in an organized way.

This idea of thinking in terms of happiness comes down to these simple truths. What you think is who you are. If you think in terms of poverty, then you will be poor. If you are thinking in terms of prosperity, then you will be prosperous. Keep your ideas and thoughts on happy and successful cycles, and you will begin to see successful results.

READ AND LISTEN TO EMPOWERING BOOKS

You always have a choice about what you listen to, read, and what you allow into your mind. If you want to develop a healthy mindset, ask yourself one simple question before you watch TV or movies, surf the internet, or do some reading:

Is what I am doing going to improve my thinking or contribute negativity to my mind?

Improving the way in which you think and making a commitment to your happiness is a decision that few are willing to make—either out of laziness or disbelief or because they do not know where to get started or who to listen to.

When I first got started on the road to improving my life, what kept me going after the initial excitement was discovering that there is a lifetime worth or personal growth books, audio books, seminars, and workshops, that I could indulge in which would allow me to continuously challenge and grow my mind.

If you want to take your life to the next level and are ready to shift your focus to the happy and motivating occurrences that happen all the time, then you definitely want to read and listen to empowering books. You want to immerse yourself in anything that will improve your mind, grow your potential, and strengthen your willpower. The same goes for friends and family. Spend the bulk of your time with people committed to developing a healthy mindset, and limit the time you spend with those who make you feel bad about yourself or make you question your power.

FIND A MASTERMIND GROUP

Have you ever noticed that it is easier to solve problems when a group of people are brainstorming and working together, rather than just doing it on your own? The idea of working together as a team is nothing new. However, in the early 1900s a gentleman by the name of Dr. Napoleon Hill (October 26, 1883 – November 8, 1970) took this idea to a much deeper level. Dr. Hill is known as the grand-daddy of the personal-success industry, made famous by his book, *Think and Grow Rich*.

In this book, Hill talks about the importance of creating a Mastermind Alliance if you want to take your professional and personal life to the next level.

> *"No mind is complete by itself. It needs contact and association with other minds to grow and expand."*

Out of respect for his incredible contribution to the human potential movement, here are two quotes from Dr. Hill that define a Mastermind Alliance.

> *"The coordination of knowledge and effort of two or more people who work together in perfect harmony for attainment of a definite purpose."*

***

LESSON FOUR: DEVELOP A HEALTHY MINDSET

"A friendly alliance with one or more persons who will encourage one to follow through with both plan and purpose."

A Mastermind Alliance is a meeting of highly focused, like-minded people who are dedicated to achieving a common goal. Each person typically has different skills that they contribute to the group. Meetings occur regularly and consist of brainstorming, problem-solving, goal-achieving, and education. Being part of a Mastermind Alliance allows each member to tap into the expertise of other members toward the achievement of a common good. What could take many years to solve as an individual could take one year or less with a Mastermind.

The reason why I am here, contributing my writing to this book, is because I was invited to be a part of a Mastermind Alliance. Without hesitation, I joined and aligned myself with the same mindset and beliefs that the group was focused on. Several of the other guys in the group were already co-authors of this book, which led me to also being invited to become one of the authors.

Being part of a Mastermind Alliance has completely changed my outlook on life. It made me realize that no matter what goes on, no matter what challenges I face or what goals I want to achieve, there is always quality, success-minded people out there to help me solve problems and move forward.

Of all the things that I have learned, at the top of the list is the importance of developing a small-knit group of people that you know and trust that you can share your goals and ideas with; a group of people that can help you further develop your plans, and give you the backup and support you need to push you in the right direction.

LESSON FIVE

TAKE RESPONSIBILITY FOR YOUR OUTCOME

"If you could kick the person in the pants responsible for most of your trouble, you wouldn't sit for a month."
— Theodore Roosevelt

Do you think it is possible to have a healthy mindset and at the same time blame people and situations for your failures? From everything I have learned since immersing myself in personal development, having a healthy mindset means taking responsibility for your outcomes. Taking responsibility can be interpreted in two ways.

- Personal responsibility: taking responsibility for your outcomes, whether it be the decisions you make or the situations you find yourself in.
- External responsibility: When you are accountable to others who depend on you to get something done, like finishing your side work before heading home from work so that everything is ready to go tomorrow.

Being known as someone who takes responsibility for your outcome is a valuable trait, because it adds credibility and likability to your character. Being reliable is also a huge part of being responsible. A person who does as promised can be considered a reliable person. Reliability is an admirable characteristic because people do not like to deal with those who are unreliable. They would rather give their energy, business, and rewards to the person they can count on. Also, the reliable person feels good knowing that he or she is trusted.

People who demonstrate personal responsibility or external responsibility have four empowering beliefs that allow them to maintain their inner-strength.

- Do not blame others
- Make peace with the past
- Be intentional
- Find your purpose

DO NOT BLAME OTHERS

One of the most destructive patterns of behavior is playing the blame game. It has been responsible for the start of wars, failed relationships, lost friendships, causing rage between drivers, court cases, and countless other controversies.

Blaming other people and situations is the easiest way to deflect personal responsibility. It happens because as a whole, people simply do not like to take the blame for their shortcomings or failures, or they do not understand how their actions or choices affected a situation.

If you are caught up in the blame game and want to shift gears and take on a greater amount of responsibility in your life, then you have to begin to own up to and take responsibility for everything that happens in your life, even events outside of your control. This does not mean you take responsibility for the things that you did not do. It means you take responsibility for how you let things affect you, and also for how you respond to situations.

When you make the leap in awareness that you are where you are in life because of your prior actions and choices, then it becomes easier to become a more responsible person.

My life started taking a quantum leap for the better when I started connecting the dots, and I saw how my decisions and actions were reflecting back to me as my life experiences. When I stopped blaming others for my challenges, I gained more control over my life, mostly because I stopped allowing myself to be influenced by outside circumstances. Instead, I started being the influencer in my own life. One of the easiest ways to stop blaming is to make peace with the past and move on.

MAKE PEACE WITH THE PAST

Have you ever met someone who is stuck in the past and is holding a grudge for the longest time and never gets over it? When you think about them, do they seem happy? Or are they negative all the time? People like this have no concept of personal responsibility. They are locked into the blame mindset.

Even though it is easy to be tempted to hold something against someone, it is more beneficial to forgive and forget and just move on. Life happens. People make mistakes. There is far more to gain from learning from a bad situation than there is from stewing on something that cannot be changed. Be responsible and learn from your mistakes as well as those of others. Try to make things better when you can, but rest content that this is an imperfect world. Do not expect perfection from others if you have not realized it within yourself.

BE INTENTIONAL

People who live responsibly know how to connect the dots. They can take any situation and look at all points of view to find the "big picture." When you can see how one event triggers another event, then this allows you to be more intentional with the situations in your life. Instead of living in reaction, you live from being creative.

Some people naturally understand how their thoughts and actions create their life. I figured this out when I learned about the Law of Attraction. According to this law, everything in the universe is slowly and steadily vibrating at its frequency. A carrot has a different vibration than a banana, and a rock has a different vibration than a tree. Our thoughts also have their frequency of vibration. Happiness, love, and forgiveness have a different frequency than anger, blame, or resentment. The Law of Attraction states that we attract into our lives whatever we are focusing on. We attract people and events that match our mental and emotional frequency.

How many times have you heard someone say, *"You reap what you sow"*? That saying is the same thing as the Law of Attraction. You sow with your thoughts and reap with your actions. Whatever you bring into this universe in terms of thought and action is reciprocated back into your life through the Law of Attraction. We attract and get what we give.

The most challenging part of accepting the truth about the Law of Attraction is coming to the realization that every single one of your experiences in life, good and bad, have been shaped by you alone. You either directly caused the situation by action or inaction, or the way you chose to look at a situation affected its outcome.

When you have a healthy, positive mindset, you attract people and situations of the same vibration pattern. The universe is rigged in your favor if you know how to intentionally manage your thoughts. A big part of being responsible is knowing how to think the right thoughts and take the right actions so that you get the results that you want.

FIND YOUR PURPOSE

Taking responsibility for your outcomes also includes giving your life meaning and purpose, and finding a definite chief aim which becomes the focal point of your life.

If you look at your life right now, do you have a long-term vision for yourself, or are you just going at it day-by-day? Are you a wandering generality or a meaningful specific? Have you set up goals and small wins to ensure you never get tired of what you are doing, or are you just going through the motions with no true vision for your future? Are you going to go to work tomorrow because you went yesterday and because they give you a paycheck? If so, is that something you want to do for the rest of your life?

A lot of people are stuck doing something they hate for the entire 40-plus years of their working life leading up to their retirement. They live an unhappy life because they failed to pursue their true passion. If you really break it down, that is 40 hours a week, for 40 years. That adds up to 83,000 hours doing something they can barely motivate themselves to wake up for.

Far too many people see their dreams and passions as a suggestion or just a "hobby." What if it did not have to be that way? What if there was a way to live your life doing what you love to do? What if you could define yourself by finding your true passion and pursuing what is important to you? What if your personal interests could fuel your dreams and desires?

I believe that one of the main reasons people do not live their passions is because they do not know how to become clear about what truly excites them, or they have not yet defined the purpose of their life. Not knowing what excites you or what the purpose of your life is would be like driving a car with no map and no destination, and you drive until you run out of fuel. Once you run out of fuel, you just sit there until you die.

If you are struggling with finding your passion or your true purpose in life, take some time to answer these questions. They will help you tune into what is truly important to you.

LESSON FIVE: TAKE RESPONSIBILITY FOR YOUR OUTCOME

- What are your two most important core values in life?
- Of these two, what is your most important core value? This is the basis of your main purpose.
- What can you do that is fun and rewarding that will fulfill your primary values?
- What are your strengths? How can you use them to feel fulfilled?
- What do you feel most passionate about that gets you up early and keeps you up late?
- What are the main emotions that you want to feel throughout your life?
- How do you want to be remembered by others when you die?
- What values do you want to pass along to your children?

To help you answer these questions, here is a partial list of core values. After you scan through this list, see if any of them match up with what is most important to you. You can also add your own to the list.

- Accountability
- Achievement
- Balance
- Community
- Compassion
- Confidence
- Contribution
- Determination
- Faith
- Family
- Growth
- Honesty
- Integrity
- Kindness
- Leadership
- Love
- Loyalty
- Respect
- Responsibility
- Success
- Trustworthiness
- Truthfulness

It is very important to know what you value most, because your values help you chart the course for your life. Values help you to
un-clutter your thinking so that you can make decisions based on what is most important to you. Values help you to decide how to respond to different situations. They also help you to decide what type of people you allow into your life because you only want people to be close to you who match your values.

Bruce Lee, the legendary actor and martial artist, had a very clear life purpose that he wrote in his early 20s and became the driving force behind his achievements.

> *I, Bruce Lee, will be the first highest-paid Oriental superstar in the United States. In return, I will give the most exciting performances and render the best of quality in the capacity of an actor. Starting in 1970, I will achieve world fame, and from then onward till the end of 1980, I will have in my possession $10,000,000. I will live the way I please and achieve inner harmony and happiness.* (Bruce Lee, 1969)

My chief aim is to become wiser and develop a greater perception of life every day so that I can add value to other people's lives.

> *I am increasing my future potential by connecting with new people every day and being positive in everything that I do. All my relationships are transforming into a new chapter in life that is more venturous and satisfying. Every day I am increasing my financial status, communication skills, and personal perseverance until there is never a doubt in my mind.*

Taking responsibility for the outcome of your life is the greatest challenge you can give to yourself. Few people have the courage to face the unknown and to make their passions and dreams become their reality. It is not always easy. It may even be more difficult at first, but in the end, it is worth the risk. The beauty of it is that when you have the right mindset, and as your life and interests change and evolve, you know how to adjust your thinking and actions to accommodate new interests and desires.

Epilogue

When I first became a co-author of this book, I did not know what I was going to write about, but I knew that I had a lot to offer. Even though I was only 18 years old, I felt like I had enough experience and insight to share what life is like from my point of view at this young age.

Working with my writing coach and mentor, David Strauss, and all the other guys who are co-authors of this book helped me to become clear about what I wanted to share. It is one thing to want to write a book, but it is a whole other thing learning how to ask yourself what you truly believe about life, and then putting those thoughts into an organized format that can help others to learn through your own experience.

My main intention in writing was to motivate others to take control of their lives. I knew that my story could benefit and inspire others, and I also felt that by writing this book, I would learn a lot more about who I am and what I am about.

Another reason why I chose to be a part of this book was to get over my self-limiting beliefs from school and to give myself the challenge to tap into my potential. I wanted to prove to myself that I am so much more than just a product of the school system. I was no superstar in school. In fact, it was the opposite. But look where that got me. That limitation became my motivation. Instead of seeing myself as just an *okay student* the rest of my life, I changed my identity and saw myself as someone who could write and share his enthusiasm for wanting to make a difference in the world.

In writing this book, there is one thing that has become very clear to me: your mind is your most valuable asset. If you learn to take control of your thoughts, feelings, and focus, your potential will skyrocket, no matter what age you are. This is especially true if you are willing to take on a coach and mentor to help you unleash that potential.

The big challenge for me when I started writing my content was choosing the most important ideas to make my main points of discussion. The five insights that I decided upon were the very steps that I had to go through to successfully write this book.

- I had to be open to making changes in my thinking and beliefs.

- I had to commit to personal growth, because when you set out on the journey of becoming an author, sharing your personal story and examining your own beliefs can be a real challenge. You learn a lot about yourself when you take the time to reflect on your life and extract the most valuable lessons.

- I had to be a coachable person, because if I wanted to do something that I had never done before, I had to open myself up to new ideas and new ways of thinking. I also had to be open to constructive feedback that helped me to get my ideas out of my heart and head and onto paper.

- I had to develop a healthy mindset. One of the benefits of writing this book was the process of examining my thoughts and beliefs and deciding what is and is not important to me. This was a huge challenge because never before had I sat down with and asked myself what I truly believed about life. Another benefit was being a part of the mastermind with all of the authors and with our coach and mentor, David Strauss.

- Most importantly, I had to take responsibility for my outcome. A lot of people talk about writing a book, but the real test was seeing this through to the finish. There were so many bogus reasons and lame excuses to quit, but with the support of our team and coach, we all kept each other accountable and pushed each other to get things done.

I tapped into the five insights because I also believe that if I can do this—if I can share my story of failures and successes—I can encourage and inspire other young kids to break out of their mold and do something extraordinary. I want people to know that their weaknesses and failures do not define them, but they give them experience and perspective to learn and grow.

Too many kids are bored with life or have not found their passion or purpose, and so they are settling with being mediocre. They have tried and failed, are afraid to get back up and try again, or they have fallen to peer pressure like I did and do not know the steps to being successful.

Those of us in our teens and 20s have the most potential out of any generation because we have all the knowledge of the world in the palm of our hands—literally, with our smartphones. If each of those kids could tap into the power of their mind and all of the lessons shared in this entire book, we could be the generation that reshapes the world.

In reading this entire book, I want people to know that the best solution to overcoming their obstacles lies solely within themselves. The amount of confidence and belief in yourself determines your success.

I want to help people overcome being scared and shy and have a new level of confidence in themselves to do whatever they desire.

It is my hope that when you consume this entire book you will make a serious shift in your thinking so that you can confidently transform your life and go after your dreams. This shift will then take you in a direction where you can thrive and grow.

It is my intention that by being honest and real with you about my life, that you will have the courage to do the same for yourself. If you go out of your way to apply the five insights, you will see phenomenal improvements in every area of your life.

After I had the realization that the direction of my life is up to me, I was able to understand better why all of my past decisions led me to where I am today. I felt at peace knowing that I am responsible for the way things turn out in my life. It all starts with taking action and realizing that it doesn't come overnight. We must be patient on our paths, because the journey is the destination in the end.

You were given life and you did nothing to deserve it. It was just a gift. Take this into account, if you were given life, how many other gifts are waiting for you to discover them? How many more blessings will come your way?

I challenge you to get to know who you are. Discover your potential. Act on your intuition. Take risks that will cause you to grow. Develop confidence, and never stop learning. All of these are gifts you can give to yourself. Receive the gifts.

Acknowledgements

I would like to give thanks to everyone who is a part of the *Think Gen Why* book for inspiring me to become one of the authors. Back in January of 2017, Eric, Jesse, Ryan, Matt, and Kyler asked me to be a part of their mastermind and to take part in this project. Never did I think that at such a young age I would become a published author. You guys have had a huge impact on my life. You have inspired and motivated me to become a better person. I will always be grateful for that.

Special thanks to David Strauss, my mentor, who also inspired me to be a part of this movement. From giving me countless hours of coaching to helping me organize my thoughts for this book, none of us could have done this without you.

Lastly, I would like to thank my parents and grandparents for raising me the way that they did. They taught me the importance of humility and patience. When I was younger, I remember when my nana would always show me and my sister's proper manners at the dinner table. Looking back on it, it is not like that was a huge lesson to be learned, but when compiled with all the other valuable guidance, it compounded over the years to make me who I am.

My parents have always been supportive over the years, pushing me to be the best I can be. I know when growing up it is easy to think that parents can be foolish, but now looking back, my parents always knew what was best for me. Thank you for doing everything in your power to ensure that we had a stable upbringing.

Every one of you is unique in your own way, and have had a significant influence on my life. I would not have been able to be a part of *Think Gen Why* without you. It is going to be so powerful to see how this book not only affects our lives as we apply what we have written, but how it will also positively affect the lives of many other kids and young adults as they learn how to take control of their situation and develop healthy habits.

BOOK SIX

DOUBLE DOWN

FOUR LESSONS TO TAKE OWNERSHIP OF YOUR LIFE

• J. ERIC WRIGHT •

Prologue

*"Winners, I am convinced, imagine their dreams first.
They want it with all their heart and expect it to come true.
There is, I believe, no other way to live."*
— *Joe Montana*

When looking at my life, many would wonder why I am writing a book. I was the kid who struggled with every English assignment ever given to him. I have failed more years of English than I passed. I was forgotten or written off by most of my teachers, and I eventually dropped out of high school only days before senior graduation.

I cannot blame my parents for my academic challenges. Just like a lot of people, I grew up in a decently successful household. I am one of five children spread out over 14 years. There are three girls, two boys, and two great parents. We rarely lived outside of our means. We always had food and money for the bills.

Things changed a little bit when my parents decided to make a change around the time I was about nine years old, and we moved into a nicer home in a better area of town with much better schools. All of us were made aware that it was going to cost a lot more to live in this new place. To make this work, my parents decided to sacrifice our family vacations, nicer cars, and trips for themselves, as well as anything they did not deem necessary for raising us. They made this choice knowing that we would have a better education and be surrounded by higher-quality people in a more positive environment. It also allowed us to excel in sports because athletics was a big part of our new school.

Unfortunately, for me, things did not work out as well as my parents had hoped. Public school was not easy for me, and I ended up dropping out senior year. I bailed on school because there was no way I was able to meet the academic requirements to graduate based on the school's standards and requirements.

I felt completely lost in the school system. I was smart but struggled to learn in the format they were teaching. When it came to writing exercises, I struggled because my thought process was moving too fast for my fingers to keep up and I would end up losing my thoughts when taking notes—leaving me frustrated and feeling inadequate. I struggled for many years thinking I was dumb and that I might not have the brightest future ahead of me.

A lot of my teachers saw me as a lost cause—just a waste of their time that they could otherwise be spending on students who could understand the information that was being taught. I cannot remember a single teacher who said you could still be successful without college. And frankly, I had teachers tell my mother and me, to our faces, that I would not be successful.

"He is just not able to focus or sit through class and is becoming a distraction to the other students."

Or

"He just might need slower classes."

To better understand why school was the absolute hardest part of my life, you have to know what was going on inside my head.

I dreaded waking up and having to go to school for eight hours, and then when I finally got home, I had another four hours of homework for the next morning. As much as I struggled with my homework, I ended up doing it because I knew that after I went to school, I could participate in sports.

Other than academics, I did not have any other problems with school. I knew what was expected of me by my peers, and I never really had issues with them. Of course, there was an occasional jerk or someone who I had a conflict with, but overall, I got along with most everyone. I liked the social aspect of school. I enjoyed hanging out with a lot of my friends. It was amazing seeing my girlfriend every day, and I loved participating in sports.

The real reason school was so tough was because of the relationships that I had with most of my teachers. Of course, I had a few teachers who I was able to build a strong relationship with. To them, I would like to give thanks, because they helped me get to where I am today. Other than them, I would say that my feelings of inadequacy in school started at a younger age, around fourth grade.

PROLOGUE

When I was about 10 years old, I had just transitioned from private school to being enrolled in public school. I went from having three or four kids in my class to twenty-five, and a total of 90 kids in my age group. You can imagine what a big jump it was for me. I struggled right off the bat because at my previous school we did not have homework. They almost did not believe in homework and rarely gave it to us unless we did not finish what we were supposed to do in class. So now, for the first time in my life, I started getting homework. And I mean every night I was getting a lot of homework, most of which was just busy work. I started falling behind my peers as I quickly discovered that my ability to read, spell, and do basic grammar was far below the average student. I was not the greatest at math, but I could hold my own. Every year I kept falling behind my peers a little bit more.

As my academic struggles progressed, I started to understand that the school thing was not really for me. I began realizing at about eighth grade that I did not want to go to college, which made it harder for me to stay focused because my school was very competitive, and they put a lot of pressure on kids to go to college. For most of the kids, that was the path that they were going to take. But to me, it felt like they did not think it was okay not to go to college, and it really weighed heavy on my self-esteem. I do not believe I had a single teacher who once said it is okay not to go to college.

Knowing at such an early age that I really was not going to have the grades or the athletic ability to go to college or get a scholarship, the only thing I could do was push myself to get decent grades so that I would be able to participate in after-school sports, which was my true passion.

Over the next few years, my academic struggles only worsened. I started falling so far behind that by my sophomore year, I had already failed some classes and was no longer eligible to play sports. This crushed me. The one reason why I endured through all my struggles with school and put up with everything that I hated about it was because I wanted to play sports. Now, the one thing that kept me sane was being taken away from me. This only worsened my feelings of inadequacy, and my motivation to go to school started dropping rapidly.

Since I could no longer play sports, I began doing my own after-school extracurricular activities. I started getting into trouble, was hanging with the wrong crowd, and began going down a slippery slope. It took me about two years to wake up—after a big slap across the face—and understand that the life that I had been living was really bad.

I ended up crawling my way to my senior year. Right around the last month of classes I was told that I was not going to be graduating with my peers, and that I would have to take another whole year of school if I wanted to get a high school diploma. At that point, I did not see any reason to stay, so I decided that I was finished with school. With only about three weeks left in my senior year, I stopped going to school because if I was not going to graduate—and I definitely was not going to attend another year of academic torture—I had no business attending the last couple of weeks.

Just a couple days after I stopped going to school, one of my good buddies, Keith, actually called me up and said, *"Hey man, I know you are not going to school anymore. I came across this business opportunity that I am going to go check out tonight you should come with me."*

I always had been an entrepreneur. I had done my fair share of lemonade stands as a kid, and when I was old enough, I always found or made work for myself. I was doing anything from mowing lawns to shoveling driveways, really, anything that I could do to make some money. I am the son of an entrepreneur, so working for myself or something similar to that intrigued me.

When Keith introduced me to this new business, of course I was interested. When we arrived at the presentation, we were on the back patio getting pitched a good old traditional multi-level (MLM) network marketing business. As the presenter, Tony Grebmeier, was speaking, he must have been able to see my facial expressions because after he was done, he walked straight over to me and began talking with me. He asked me about my story and what I had been through. I explained to him that I was not going to be attending college and that I was not going to graduate high school. I told him that I was in a pretty tough spot. He said that he understood what that felt like and asked if I was interested in this concept. I told him I was and that I would be looking for a mentor if I decided to do this. He told me that I could follow him, and that was the day that forever changed my life.

He took me under his wing, spending a lot of time pouring his life experiences and wisdom into me, teaching me as much as he could about how to be successful. This knowledge allowed me to leap forward a couple of years in maturity which, in return, put me in a position to start surrounding myself with people who had the same wants, desires, and aspirations as me.

I was lucky enough to find another mentor, in addition to Tony, who shared some powerful advice.

PROLOGUE

> *"If you want to succeed in life, find somebody who has what you want, do what they do, say what they say, and you'll get what they got—every single time."*

I spent all those years in school, and never did a single teacher share such an important piece of wisdom for success.

I did exactly what I was told. I found somebody who had what I wanted—a successful family, a successful business, and an overall successful life. I started doing what he did and saying what he said, and I started seeing some of the same results that he had. After seeing some success, I started to give back to kids my age by teaching them the same lessons that had been taught to me. I started feeling like a leader, which then allowed me to move forward in my business and opened my horizon to what was truly possible for my talents and potential.

Being introduced to Tony and his leadership in the MLM business forced me to step out of my comfort zone and start growing. I began reading a lot of business and self-help books, going to personal growth and entrepreneurial seminars, meeting cool people who positively influenced me and encouraged me to keep growing into the young man I am today.

Even though many of my teachers saw me as hopeless, I had finally found the people and situations that were teaching me the way I like to learn while giving me a sense of purpose and a taste of success.

It has been about five years since I first met Tony and was introduced to the world of personal development. Now that I have been surrounded by so many successful people and have done a lot of entrepreneurial learning on my own, I have developed patterns of thinking that have formed the foundation for my new approach to life. I am no longer the kid who dropped out of high school, and I no longer look down upon myself. I also know that there are plenty of other guys and gals who can relate to my struggles, so I have simplified the key points of what I have learned thus far into four lessons which anyone can use to clean up their thinking and improve the quality of their life.

- Cultivate a family environment
- Double down on what you're good at
- When the going gets tough, get focused
- Turn challenges into opportunities

LESSON ONE

CULTIVATE A FAMILY ENVIRONMENT

"The best way to predict the future is to create it."
— *Peter Drucker*

Have you ever noticed how much people want to belong to or be a part of something? This goes all the way back to school when we wanted to be accepted by our peers, or find that right group of people that we fit into. It does not end with school. I have noticed that people of all ages want to feel like they are a part of something bigger than themselves. They want to feel liked and loved by others, to feel connected, significant, and valued and have a sense of purpose and meaning for their life.

I believe that this *need* to be a part of something is one of the most important observations I have made because it has shown me that the best way to build a team or business, or even relationships, is by cultivating a family environment. I have to give credit to my parents for this observation because they did the best they could to cultivate a family environment. When I look back upon what I learned and observed, for me, creating a family environment means nurturing four supportive habits which cultivate a sense of belonging.

1) Be a good listener
2) Acknowledge strengths and weaknesses
3) Challenge people to learn and grow
4) Give acknowledgement and praise

Be a Good Listener

People want to be heard, and they want to know that you care. When you listen to others, you give them a sense of belonging. Whether or not you agree with what someone says, when they are done talking, thank them for sharing their point of view.

Acknowledge Strengths and Weaknesses

If you see someone doing something wrong or acting inappropriately, compliment one of their strengths first, and then point out where they are out of line. For example: *"John, you are a really smart guy, I am not quite sure how you made this mistake. Let's figure this out together so that next time we can get it right."*

Challenge People to Learn and Grow

Do not accept mediocrity from yourself or others. Challenge people to improve their lives by encouraging them to get out of their comfort zone and put their potential to the test.

Give Acknowledgement and Praise

Anyone can find fault. It takes real heart to notice what is good about a person or situation. Make sure you regularly make a point of acknowledging peoples' wins and praise their accomplishments. Make sure you give your praise lavishly so that people recognize you as someone who cares about others and notices their best qualities.

There are lots of different ways to cultivate a family environment, but I see these as the basics that will pay huge dividends in the quality of your relationships. Plus, when you treat others well, the good returns to you tenfold.

Cultivating a family environment starts with cleaning up your own environment so that you can be a role model for others. You have to always be working on improving your thinking, raising your standards, and expanding your awareness. Here are five winning strategies for cleaning up your environment.

1) Surround yourself with the right people
2) Develop a Support system for yourself
3) Create a supportive culture
4) Establish a team mindset
5) Raise your standards

LESSON ONE: CULTIVATE A FAMILY ENVIRONMENT

SURROUND YOURSELF WITH THE RIGHT PEOPLE

Inspirational author and motivational speaker Jim Rohn famously said that *"We are the average of the five people we spend the most time with."* No truer words have ever been spoken. I model my life based on this advice. If you want to apply this same thinking to your life, you have to be willing to step back and take a close look at the people in your life. When taking inventory, you have to group people into two different categories, positive or negative, so that you can see their impact on your life.

Positive people are people who are uplifting when you get around them. They make you feel good. These are the people that when they call you, you get excited to answer the phone. They are there for you when you need them, and are consistently reliable.

Negative people, on the other hand, are the ones who drag you down whenever you talk with them. They may be needy, are always blaming or looking for excuses, or have a doom-and-gloom outlook on life. You dread when they call because you do not want their energy to affect your day. When dealing with negative people, very rarely will your positive energy influence them because they will always default back to their negative mindset.

Below is a cool chart that breaks things down a bit more. You can add your own qualities and your own friends and family, but this will help you to visualize the ideal people to keep in your life.

Qualities	John	Mary	Susan	Peter	Scott	Amanda
People who depend on you		*				*
People you depend upon	*		*	*		
Positive mindset	*		*		*	*
Negative mindset		*		*	*	
Taker						*
Giver	*	*	*	*		
Respectful	*	*	*	*	*	*
Disrespectful					*	
Reliable	*	*	*			
Unreliable		*		*	*	*
Lazy		*				*
Self-motivated	*		*	*		
Etc...						

When you take inventory, it does not mean get rid of everybody in your life or even start tossing people out. It means taking an honest look at the direction you are taking your life and deciding who fits in. Some people you may choose to keep in your life, but on a smaller scale. Others may not belong in your life at all, and the best of the best you may choose to spend more time with.

Develop a Support System for Yourself

Cultivating a family environment also means that you have to develop a support system for yourself so that you can be your best. Some people believe that asking for help or looking for support means you are weak. If you grew up in a non-supportive environment, it may seem foreign to you to ask for help because it was never there for you. Somehow you need to let go of any stigma, shame, or guilt that you associate with asking for help.

Through everything I have recently learned from reading books, going to seminars, and talking with my mentors, successful people make a habit of getting help and support from others, and they do it strategically instead of by knee-jerk reactions. They understand that there is no shame in needing help, but they take it to a higher standard than most people. They know that you should only ask for help or support from people who have the awareness or results that you want. They also know the value of creating a support system for yourself so that you always have access to reliable people in times of need.

When you are ready to create a support system for yourself, you have to identify the people who you can rely on. This is the group of people that you could fall back on at a moment's notice when things get rough, or you need help or advice. Think of it this way: the number one determining factor of who will show up at your funeral is the weather. You want your support group to be the people who will show up on your last day above ground, regardless of the weather. If you were stranded on the road 20 miles away at three o'clock in the morning, who would you call? The individuals you would call to come and help are what I like to call your inner circle, or your support system.

Your support system should include people you can rely upon for financial advice, career advice, relationship advice, and just general insight into life's challenges and opportunities. Some of these people may already be in your life, or you may need to seek out and develop friendships with people who can fill those shoes.

Create a Supportive Culture

Once you have identified your support system, it is time to flip the coin and be that person for others. This is important when creating a family environment because when you treat people like family, you learn how to give and receive.

When you put yourself in a position of leadership and support for others, it is important to keep in mind that when people come to you for support or advice, they may be making life-decisions based on what you say. Be sincere, and only provide guidance in areas that you do know your stuff. Some people may come to you just because they like you, but that doesn't mean you have the answer for them. It is okay to set boundaries and say, *"I'm sorry, I am not the right person to answer that question. Maybe it would be better to get advice from someone with more experience."*

Ask yourself this question. When people talk about you, what do you want them to say—good things or bad things? Ideally, I would think that you want people to say that you are very strong, supportive, caring, encouraging, and reliable.

When you develop into being a supportive person, it is going to show up in how you relate to people at work, your friendships, family, and people you are closest with. You need to know how to set boundaries in each of those areas, especially when it comes to work because at work, you do not want your kindness to be confused with being tolerant of poor performance.

In a work situation, you must handle things differently by using a lot more discernment when you talk with people. You have to make sure that you keep it a safe place for people to be real, but also that they know that you have to make decisions based on the best interests of the business. Besides, when you are strong and have integrity, people will respect you even more, and that is how growth happens. People will grow and become stronger and more loyal when you challenge them in an uplifting way to perform better.

One of the biggest signs of being a part of a supportive culture is when you feel like the people you look up to for advice are approachable, and they are always looking for win-win solutions instead of over-emphasizing the problems. When you set people up to win and support their success, they will treasure your presence in their life.

Establish a Team Mindset

One of the most important traits to have when building a family environment is transparency. This means being open, upfront, and honest with everyone you communicate with. Transparency leaves no doubt and allows trust to be built in a much faster timeline. The more transparent you are, the less that comes to light later. One of the things I appreciate about my parents is that they were very transparent with us kids, especially when it came to big decisions that affected the entire family. Because of this, there was a lot of love and trust.

One of my favorite stories to teach the value of transparency and its importance in establishing a team mindset is the story of King Arthur's roundtable. Not only did King Arthur see every one of the Knights as unique individuals, he also saw them as equals. He fashioned a table that was round so that everyone would have an equal say—no man was superior over any other. They all had different fighting styles to bring to the table. They had a code of honor they followed, and they decided that they were never going to complete a mission if it went against their morals. They always chose family first and money second. Their moral compass demanded that they do what was right even though sometimes it was not what they favored. They understood that one person can ruin the honor of the entire group, so they exercised tremendous discernment in whom they allowed to enter the table.

The high moral standards of King Arthur and his knights may seem unrealistic nowadays, but only to those people who do not value honor and integrity. What is crucial to understand is that you cannot cultivate a family environment without establishing a team mindset, which is based on honesty and integrity.

Raise Your Standards

Cultivating a family environment is more than just treating people well. It is also about continuously raising your standards about what is and is not acceptable in your life, while at the same time lifting people up so that everyone can become a better person and tap into their potential. Knowing my challenges with my traditional education, the only way I was going to improve my life was by raising my standards. One thing I knew for sure: having low self-esteem and seeing myself as being a failure was not acceptable. One of the first things I did was raise my standards by becoming very teachable. I knew that with an open mind and a high willingness to learn, anything is possible.

Most people do not even realize that they have standards, but we all do. We have standards for the people we allow into our lives, for the type of food we eat, the clothes we wear, the car we drive, and the home we live in. For far too many people, their standards are based on what they can afford, not realizing that if they raise their standards, they can eventually have nicer things in their life if they are committed to being teachable and discovering new ways of thinking.

When it comes to cultivating a family environment, the most important standard to set is how you will communicate with each other. Nothing breaks down cohesion and community faster than poor communication. The worst culprits are making assumptions, jumping to conclusions, and overreacting.

We have all heard the saying "monkey-see, monkey-do." Whatever you do in front of others, they will deem as acceptable. If you set high standards, the people in your *family* will follow in your tracks. If they do not want to have higher standards, they will sort themselves out.

Tony Robbins, one of the world's foremost thought leaders, has a quote that says:

> *"You don't always get what you want,
> but you always get what you need."*

When you raise your standards, you get a new list of needs. You start to expect more of yourself and others, and you do not settle for anything less than what is deemed acceptable. People will mirror your confidence if you believe in yourself and them, and they will believe in themselves, too. When you get a full buy-in on this from your *family,* you can count it as a win.

LESSON TWO

DOUBLE DOWN ON WHAT YOU ARE GOOD AT

*"Success is achieved by developing our strengths,
not by eliminating our weaknesses."*
— Marilyn vos Savant

When I look back at my school days with my new, entrepreneurial mind, I realize that the school system was asking me to be something that I am not. I was never the guy to sit in the front row, take good notes, study hard and kick ass on my exams. The school saw me as broken and wanted to fix me, but they could not because I was not broken.

We are taught in school to always get better at what we are bad at. My teachers wanted to fix my weaknesses, but they did not take the time to figure out my strengths and what I was good at. I was a mess in school because they had me double down on the wrong thing.

The issue with the approach to education is that it is outdated. We do not live in the same society that the schools are preparing us for. Technology has started to connect us in ways never thought possible before. It was barely over 20 years ago (1996) when email became a mainstream reality with Hotmail. Instant messaging was just coming on board shortly after that. Now, today, you can communicate with somebody in Africa instantaneously. With the globalization of the world and technology advancing as fast as it is, it no longer makes sense for people to spend time getting better at things they are not good at. My school would have served me better if they helped me to discover my passion and how to tap into it with today's technology.

When you enter the business world and begin to work, you start to realize the importance of specialization. Sometimes doubling down on what you are good at allows you to make more money and bring more value to the marketplace than you could have if you had spent that same time trying to improve in areas where you are not as talented.

The entrepreneurial way of thinking is completely different than what is taught in school. If you have an idea for a business that you want to build, you do not have to have the skills to build the business. All you need to have is a clear vision of what you want to create, and then hire the right people who have the talents and skills to make your dream become a reality. When you hire people, you are leveraging their talents so that you can focus your energy on what you are good at. As an entrepreneur, the best skill to have is to be a talent scout. If you can become an expert at finding experts, you can build anything.

When you double down on what you are good at, it does not mean you stop learning. It means you focus your attention on how to raise your standards of what you are good at so that you can keep getting better. If you want to learn something new that fits into your way of thinking, that is a plus, but never change who you are so that you can fit into someone else's mold. There are always going to be things that you need to do that you do not like or are not great at, especially as an entrepreneur. You just do not want to get lost in those things and neglect what you are good at. Make sure you know when to hire the right talent.

The trick to doubling down is to be aware of your weaknesses, know your strengths, and play your strengths. If you apply this thinking to a business, you will create organizations stacked with high performing people. This does not mean you should ignore your weaknesses. If you are lousy at communicating, you definitely want to take steps to improve in that area. If you do not know how to take care of your health, you need to learn because no one else can take care of your body for you. Basically, you have to develop discernment about where you should improve yourself, and where it is best to hire talent.

When you are ready to double down on what you are good at, here are six questions to ask yourself that will get you fired up.

1) What are you good at?
2) How can you get better?
3) What can you do with your best skills?

4) What is holding you back?
5) How can you leverage your weaknesses?
6) What are your opportunity costs?

What Are You Good at?

When I asked myself this question originally, the first thing that popped into my head was all the things that I was not good at. All of my life I had been made continuously aware of my weaknesses, to the point that I had a very hard time trying to come up with things that I felt I was good at. I was always so caught up on doubling down on what I was not good at so that I could meet the expectations of the school system that I had no idea who I was or what my strengths were. One of the things that I did to get over this was to ask the people who were closest to me what they felt I was the best at. To my surprise, I happen to be good at a lot of things I did not realize.

I am sure that I am not the only person in this situation. Lots of people are so busy trying to make things work in their life that they have no time to think about what are their unique strengths and interests. Think about how different our world would be if we were taught at a young age how to discover our strengths and interests and focus on those throughout our life. People would probably be a lot happier and more productive.

How Can You Get Better?

Once you have identified the skills you are good at, put together a plan on how to improve. The easiest way to improve is to reverse engineer your plan. Figure out the outcome you want, and then work backward and break down the steps you need to take to get there.

The easiest and fastest way to reverse engineer something is to find someone who has already learned how to do what you want to do and has gotten the results that you want to get. They can teach you the steps you need to take, and then all you have to do is be teachable, and be willing to learn and take action. This is exactly what I did. Once I confirmed that I wanted to be an entrepreneur, I found mentors who taught me how to clean up my thinking so that I could change my habits and behaviors, and then make decisions like an entrepreneur. I even did it with this book. Writing was not my strength, but I have always had good ideas. I finally found a writing coach and mentor, David Strauss, who was willing to help me organize my thoughts so that I can get them into book format. My strength was my creativity and quick thinking. I doubled down on that, and David helped with the rest.

What Can You Do With Your Best Skills?

When asking yourself this question, you have to be real with yourself. Self-awareness is extremely important in this step. Just because you are good at something does not mean you will always enjoy it.

I have found that finding the best outlet for doing what you truly enjoy gives you the greatest feeling of fulfillment. It also allows you to push forward and keep going when the times get hard. For example, if you love speaking and inspiring people but do not like public speaking, you may be able to find a stage for your voice through social media.

The easiest way to identify what you can do with your best skills and how to enjoy doing it is to simply write down what you like to do and then jot down all the different ways that you can do it. When you are done with that list, just choose the areas that would be the most fun for you.

What Is Holding You Back?

When you finally figure out your best skills and strengths, you have to be realistic and understand that you may not hit a home run overnight. You still have to go through the ranks of learning and improving every day.

No matter how excited you get about your newly found self-awareness, odds have it that something will hold you back. This can be normal, so do not become frustrated. A lot of people hesitate before trying something new. You just do not want your hesitation to turn into fear.

To be fair, we all come up with a lot of reasons and justifications for what is holding us back. Some people blame their environment, while others say lack of time or they do not know the right people.

If you are feeling hesitant and do not know what it is that is holding you back, change the question from *"What is holding you back?"* to *"Who is holding you back?"* One of the harder lessons to learn is that sometimes there are people in your life who are holding you back, and you have to get them out of your life for you to reach your goals. These people can be friends, family, co-workers, or anyone who drops negativity into your life.

When you remove people from your life, you are acknowledging that not everybody who is in this theme park called earth is trying to ride the same ride as you. And that's okay! The question is not whether or not you like or love your friends. You do this because you love yourself enough to make room for your dreams to become a reality. It starts with identifying what is holding you back and then cutting it loose.

How Can You Leverage Your Weaknesses?

Everyone has weaknesses—even Superman. Your weaknesses are things that de-energize you. Your strengths are things that get you excited and energized. Your weaknesses or strengths can be people, places, or situations. Look back on your life and think about what type of situations you want to avoid or that make you feel bored or frustrated. These are your weaknesses. The things that get you excited and motivated are your strengths. The ideal scenario is to do more of what you enjoy and less of what de-energizes you. Leveraging your weaknesses is the sure way to do less of what you do not like to do.

One of the easiest ways for you to leverage your weaknesses is to find somebody whose strengths are your weaknesses, and either pay them or partner up with them. This could be win-win because there is a chance that their weaknesses are your strengths and you could both benefit each other.

Here is a glimpse of a few ways to leverage your weaknesses.

- If you despise keeping track of your finances, hire a bookkeeper or accountant.
- If you are not good at keeping your place clean, you may want to hire a housekeeper.
- If you have great ideas but are not good at implementing them, retain a marketing strategist.

A lot of people waste way too much time and potential trying to get better at something that comes naturally to somebody else. In today's world, with the internet and communication in the palm of your hand, it does not make sense to waste your most valuable asset—time—to get better at something that somebody else is already great at.

What Is Your Opportunity Cost?

For a lot of people, the main reason they have learned to leverage their weaknesses and double down on what they are good at is because they understand the opportunity cost is too high if they do not. Opportunity cost is one of the most crucial things to understand when it comes to learning how to make decisions. Even though it is an economic principle, it pertains to all of life. Quite simply, it is the benefit, value, or experience that you give up when you choose to take an alternative course of action.

Every decision you make takes you away from the possibility of another opportunity. If you choose one job over another, the opportunity cost is the possible benefits and rewards of the other job. If you decide to work extra-long hours instead of going on a vacation, the opportunity cost is the vacation. If you decide not to leverage your weaknesses, the opportunity cost is the success and rewards that you would have gained had you focused on your strengths.

For me, the opportunity cost of me not graduating from high school was that I did not get an official high school diploma. What I have gained in entrepreneurial awareness and success training far outweighs the opportunity cost of not getting my diploma. I also gained the insight that I am responsible for my happiness and success.

With this idea of opportunity cost in mind, before you make decisions, if you can learn to weigh the possible gains and losses of your choices, you will be ahead of the game and set yourself up to win. By following your highest good, you will start to see that every new situation always spawns more opportunities.

LESSON THREE

WHEN THE GOING GETS TOUGH, GET FOCUSED

*"Focus on your strengths, not your weaknesses.
Focus on your character, not your reputation.
Focus on your blessings, not your misfortunes."*
— *Roy T. Bennett*

Have you ever noticed that when things get rough, some people run and hide from their problems, while others face their challenges head-on and take responsibility for the outcomes?

Ever since leaving school and working on my personal development I have noticed that people who are successful have a high level of situational awareness. They can look at everything that is going on in their life and make decisions about what is and is not working. They face life head-on. When the going gets tough, they reflect, re-evaluate, and get focused.

I have noticed five behaviors that allow successful people to get focused and ahead in their game.

1) Accept 100% responsibility for your results
2) Expand your self-awareness
3) Clarify what you want
4) Create a massive action plan
5) Reward your wins

ACCEPT 100% RESPONSIBILITY FOR YOUR RESULTS

When something happens in your life that is painful or disruptive, you have two choices. You can look for a person or situation outside of yourself to blame for what is going on, or you can accept responsibility. Guess which one has a better outcome.

You would think that it would be common knowledge that accepting responsibility is the most empowering, but surprisingly very few people understand this concept. When you do come to understand it, this concept allows you to be able to take unquestionable control of your life because you no longer live your life bound by the chains of excuses.

Accepting 100% responsibility for your results can occur in one of two ways. In the first scenario, you acknowledge that something is your fault; that it is your actions or inactions that created the situation, and you own it and do not blame anyone or anything for the conditions that arose. In the second scenario, you may or may not accept ownership for what has happened, but you understand that you have a choice of how to look at the situation and what it means to you. Instead of being a victim of circumstances, you choose to look for what you can learn from what happened and the good that can come out of it.

People who accept 100% responsibility for the results and conditions in their life typically understand that they are a magnet that is constantly attracting the same energy that they are putting off. If something negative occurs in their life or they see a recurring pattern of behavior and results, the question they ask themselves is not, *"Why is this happening?"* The question is, *"What am I doing to attract or create this?"*

Highly successful people tend to take the concept of personal responsibility to a much higher level. When faced with disruptive situations, they take responsibility for things that are truly not their fault. They do this because they understand that simply by being involved in a situation means that somehow their prior choices and decisions put them in that situation, and so they accept responsibility. Perhaps they could have communicated or explained things differently, which could have altered or prevented the outcome, or helped to avoid the undesirable results.

No matter what the situation, there is always plenty of responsibility to be taken when something goes wrong and very few hands go up to take the responsibility. The people who have the mindset of, *"When the going gets tough, get focused,"* are usually the first to step up and accept responsibility. They are the ones who understand that you cannot change anything if you blame outside circumstances because when you blame, you give your power away to affect change.

I truly believe that this concept of personal responsibility is one of the hardest things to master because it is a learned behavior. Just as you can learn to blame other people and situations, with the right frame of mind you can learn to take responsibility when things happen to you. By applying this concept to your life, when faced with challenges, it allows you to recalculate and create a new game plan to continue going forward.

Whether I realized it at the time or not, the day I dropped out of school was one of the first times I applied this concept. When I was in school, I was definitely of the *blame* mindset. The day I made that decision I began my shift in thinking. I chose to walk away from a toxic situation and expand my awareness so that I could eventually become the man I saw myself becoming.

EXPAND YOUR SELF-AWARENESS

When the going gets tough, and you want to get focused, solve problems, and get new results, you have to be willing to expand your awareness. You cannot use the same level of thinking to get out of a sticky situation that you used to get into the situation. Expanding your self-awareness is the only solution. Taking responsibility is obviously the first step, but you also have to be self-reflective and ask yourself questions that will help you to become aware of what is causing the undesirable situation so that you do not repeat it. You also have to ask questions that help you to make better choices. Here are a few questions that will help you to self reflect.

- How can I clean up my thinking?
- What wrong assumptions did I make?
- How can I make better decisions next time?
- Who can I get good advice from?
- What do I need to focus on?
- What distractions do I need to eliminate?

Expanding your self-awareness allows you to solve problems, but it can also be a preemptive measure to prevent the situation from recurring in the future. If you are the type of person who dares to face your problems head-on and gets focused, you can use your adversities as learning experiences so that you do not repeat past mistakes. You learn from your past by becoming familiar with your behavioral habits and patterns, and what you should not be doing in certain situations to avoid outcomes you do not want.

Learning how to expand my self-awareness is what saved my life. From the moment that I was introduced to personal development until now, I have been completely focused on improving my mind, cleaning up my thinking, and defining who I am. The day I dropped out of school, things were looking rough, but my life is now a testimony to the power of focus, personal responsibility, and expanded awareness.

CLARIFY WHAT YOU WANT

One of the biggest challenges to staying focused when the going gets tough is to stay committed to your outcome. Too many people lose sight of their goals and ambitions and quit when things do not go as planned. They do this because they do not know one of the basic principles of success.

Obstacles are not there to block your path or to take you off course. They are part of the path.

Imagine you are on a plane taking off from Los Angeles, heading over the Pacific Ocean to Australia. After the plane takes off, it will face tremendous resistance from turbulence, heavy winds, rain, snow, clouds, birds or countless other obstacles which push it off course. Despite all of these adverse conditions, most flights arrive at their correct destination at the intended time. The reason they arrive at their final destination is because pilots know that there will be challenges. Through help from air traffic control and internal guidance systems, they are constantly correcting their course.

Compare a flight path to your path of success. After a plane takes off, it not only gains altitude but also must start to immediately adjust its flight pattern to account for disturbances. It has to continuously recalculate its course because any wrong course correction, especially in the beginning steps, can take the flight way off course. When you first launch your pursuit of a goal, just like a plane, you have to create that initial momentum. Rarely do things go as planned, so you have to be ready, willing, and able to make adjustments to your strategy as you move forward. If you do not pay attention to the turbulence and adjust your strategy, you will find yourself completely off course. This does not mean that you will not reach your goal. It just might take you longer, especially if your goal is in the distant future.

The mistake that most people make is when they are off course, or turbulence shows up in their business or personal life, they become discouraged and allow their emotions to get in the way of their ambitions, and they lose track of their focus. Airplanes do not land to recalculate their course. They do it while they are moving at altitude. When the going gets tough, if you want to stay focused on your outcome you must develop a mindset and strategy for continuously calculating and recalculating your position. You have to be self-aware of what is going on right now, in the moment, and accept responsibility for any adverse conditions, and then clarify what you want so that you can regain your focus and stay on course. As soon as you regain focus and are honest about your situation and your surroundings, you can create a massive action plan to re-chart your course so that you can move forward. The key is to always be moving forward. From that point forward, you recalculate your path as needed.

CREATE A MASSIVE ACTION PLAN

When you are starting something new or getting back on track, you need to create a massive action plan to get your idea moving. A massive action plan is like the filing of a flight plan. It is a detailed plan of where you are going, what you are going to do, and when you are going to do it. It allows you to get the plane ready for pre-flight checks and get permission to get the plane off the ground. Once you clarified your path to your destination, gathered all the essential tools, fuel, and people, that you need to help you reach your destination, you line up on the runway, put the plane in full-throttle, and take massive action to get the plane off the ground.

Airplanes use up about 50% of their fuel on take-off because it takes an enormous amount of energy to create the initial momentum. In life, it takes an enormous concentrated effort to create the initial momentum in a new direction. A well thought-out, massive action plan will allow you to take effective action so that you minimize losses and maximize gains. The clearer you are about where you want to go and how you want to get there, the less energy it takes to get things started.

When you take massive action, it does not guarantee results. It only gets things started. The way to check-in and see if you are staying on course is to measure your results. This is true in business and personal endeavors. People who succeed keep track of their progress and measure their results. Doing so allows you to recalculate your path and change your direction when your desired results are not showing up.

In my own life, I have been in massive action mode since the day I discovered how to take responsibility for my happiness and success. When I discovered there is an entire universe of personal growth books, audiobooks, live seminars, coaches, and mentors, I took massive action to immerse myself in anything and everything I could learn to improve my life. One of the best parts of getting focused when the going gets tough is enjoying the rewards for your wins.

REWARD YOUR WINS

I do not know of anyone who works for the sake of working. We are all looking for some outcome for our efforts. It is way too easy to just keep working on yourself and your goals, and never enjoy the journey of getting there.

If you are going to go through all the effort to stay focused on your goals, make sure you become an expert at celebrating your wins. Every time you acknowledge your success, you build your confidence and create even more fire to stoke the fuel of your ambitions.

LESSON FOUR

TURN CHALLENGES INTO OPPORTUNITIES

*"What the caterpillar sees as the end of its life,
God sees as a butterfly."*
— David Lloyd Strauss

When something bad happens in your life do you feel sorry for yourself, or do you look for the win?

A lot of people do not realize this, but some people consider themselves to be winners even when they lose because they know something good can come out of any situation. Having this *winner's* mindset is priceless. It keeps you teachable because if you are one who always looks for the benefit of a difficult situation, you have to be willing to learn and view life from a different perspective.

A good example in my life of this *winner's* mindset is my solar story, which is still a work-in-progress. It all started when I was 22 years old. I came upon an income opportunity with some friends to sell solar electric installations for homes. Within two months of starting to work with the company, we left our jobs with this company to move on and create our own company. The first few weeks with our own company were pretty bumpy, but we quickly figured things out over the next couple months, and we started producing a solid amount of sales. Unfortunately, the teacher from the school of hard knocks showed up, and we had to switch companies again. It was one of the roughest years of my life because my income went on a rollercoaster ride as did my ambition. But the amount I learned and the people I met were priceless.

A large amount of what I learned was how *not* to do business. Some of the crucial lessons are:

- Always get agreements in writing: When it comes to money, expectations, responsibilities, or commitments, make sure they are in writing so that you can avoid misunderstandings.

- Set clear expectations from the beginning: Make sure everyone is on the same page and knows what they should and should not be doing.

- Do not make assumptions: If you assume something about a person or situation, verify it before you act on the assumption.

- Behave and do business with integrity: Maintain high moral standards because even if you lose some money or things go wrong, you still can sleep at night.

With these lessons in mind, I have put together four guidelines for turning challenges into opportunities.

1) You decide what things mean to you
2) Have a liquid mindset
3) You decide when to quit or keep going
4) Destroy destructive habits

YOU DECIDE WHAT THINGS MEAN TO YOU

The reason you can turn challenges into opportunities is that you decide what things mean to you. Life events are neutral; you are the one assigning meaning to what happens to you. You set the value of every situation and experience. You choose what to look for and focus on.

Every situation that causes you to get upset, happy, frustrated, excited, or disappointed, affects your emotions because you build a certain level of expectation of the outcome, and your emotions match your expectations. When you learn how to look for the opportunity in every situation, you not only get peace of mind, but you also control your emotions better because you are responding to events instead of reacting to them.

Here is a quote from one of my mentors, Jim Rohn, who speaks strongly on the importance of taking responsibility for the meaning you give to life events.

LESSON FOUR: TURN CHALLENGES INTO OPPORTUNITIES

"The wind of adversity blows on us all, but it is not the wind that's important; it is the set of the sail."

You can use that wind as an excuse, or you can use it as fuel to push you further.

HAVE A LIQUID MINDSET

When growing up as a little kid, one of my favorite movie stars was Bruce Lee. I mostly just liked him because he made crazy sounds and he was a good fighter. It was not until I got older and saw a video of one of his interviews that I realized how wise of a man he was.

In the interview, he was being asked about his mindset. In simple words, he stated:

"You must be shapeless, formless, like water. When you pour water in a cup, it becomes the cup. When you pour water in a bottle, it becomes the bottle. When you pour water into a teapot, it becomes the teapot. Water can drip, and it can crash. Become like water, my friend."

What I took from this quote is that you have to have a liquid mindset. You cannot be rigid in your thinking. You have to be adaptable to all situations. When you have a liquid mindset, no obstacle can truly stop you. It might be able to hold you back temporarily, like a dam, but eventually, even a dam cannot hold back water forever.

There is no element on earth more powerful than water. It is the gentlest, yet most devastating force that we have on this earth. It can solve problems, or it can cause problems. If you want to be the type of person who can find the opportunity in every challenge, you have to have a liquid mindset.

YOU DECIDE WHEN TO QUIT OR KEEP GOING

One of the biggest challenges that comes with looking for the opportunity hidden behind adversity is knowing when to quit or keep going. There is no doubt that if you know how to think and look long-term, you can find a positive outcome for any situation. However, that does not mean you have to stick with something that is not working. Sometimes the good that you see comes from walking away and starting something entirely new, unique, and different.

I am not one of those guys who believes that you can never quit anything. Times change, and so do people. If you have done your best to make a bad situation work, and it is not going to happen, there is no shame or loss of pride from walking away. It is pointless to waste your time, energy, money, or resources on something that will never evolve into what you thought it was going to become.

Everything has its lifespan. There is a time and a place for everything, but you cannot wait for everything to be perfect, and you cannot make things happen that are not meant to be.

> *"Those who stand at the threshold of life always waiting for the right time to change are like the man who stands at the bank of a river, waiting for the water to pass so he can cross on dry land."*
> —Joseph B. Wirthlin

A lot of people believe that by giving up on a commitment or dream, they have failed. Instead of getting out of a sinking ship they stay in because they think it is the only vehicle that is going to help them reach their goals and aspirations.

When I was in school, I was on a sinking ship. I took a leap of faith, got out, and discovered that there is always another path to follow. The road never ends, it just zigzags and goes on forever. Just because you cannot see the road ahead does not mean it is not there. You have to develop the insight and intuition to know when to keep going and when to quit.

Realistically, there are no bad choices because if you have a liquid mindset and you know how to look for the opportunity in every situation, you will always find or create the next turn in the road.

DESTROY DESTRUCTIVE HABITS

One of the biggest challenges people face is like a thief in the night, robbing you of your potential. It is not something that you can see, smell, taste or touch. It is lurking in your subconscious mind, masqueraded as your personality. It is none other than the habits that control your life.

Everyone has habits. Some peoples' habits are so ingrained in how they think that they think that they do not even recognize them as habits. They can be physical behaviors or patterns of thinking that are beneficial or detrimental to progress. Negative habits are like weeds that will not go away. Once something has roots, it is harder to pull from the ground. It is a lot easier to pull a weed than to cut down a tree.

Some of your habits may be obvious to you. If you want to know what your not-so-obvious habits are, look at the results that are showing up in your life, because your results are a measure of your habitual patterns of thinking and action.

LESSON FOUR: TURN CHALLENGES INTO OPPORTUNITIES

If you are not happy with the way your life is unfolding and want to make changes, you have to take on the challenge of changing your habits. In my family, we call this breaking the cycle of generational habits.

Generational habits are learned from the people closest to you when you are growing up. They are passed down subconsciously from one generation to the next until the pattern is broken. Sometimes the results are good; sometimes they're tragic.

Here are a few examples of dysfunctional generational habits.
- If money was tight when you were growing up, you might develop a scarcity mindset.
- If there was a lack of affection when growing up, you might have challenges with intimacy.
- If there was any physical, mental, or emotional abuse in your childhood, you might experience challenges with addiction or low self-esteem.
- If you had helicopter parents who overprotected you, you might grow up to be shy or unsure of yourself.

Just by these few examples, you can see how generational habits can evolve into more problematic behaviors as you grow up.

You break generational habits first by becoming aware of them, and then by replacing them with empowering behaviors. Where a lot of people go wrong is when they try to drop a habit cold-turkey, which rarely works. Habits meet emotional needs, and so if you drop the habit without replacing it with something beneficial, the old pattern will likely return.

What I have learned from a lot of successful people and implemented into my own life is to break old habits gently by slowly replacing them with new behaviors. It is sort of like weaning a baby off of a pacifier. If you take the pacifier away, suddenly the baby cries and whines. But if you take it away slowly and replace it with something better, it slowly adapts.
Here is one of my favorite quotes on this topic:

> *"You never change things by fighting the existing reality.*
> *To change something, build a new model that makes*
> *the existing model obsolete."*
> — R. Buckminster Fuller

Following in the tone of this quote, if you see habits in your life that are holding you back, instead of seeing them as problems to overcome, see them as opportunities to learn and grow. Develop the belief in yourself that you can always create new and better habits that will propel you further along in your life's journey.

Epilogue

When I dropped out of high school, the last thing I would have thought is that I would become a published author in my early 20s. It was probably the last thing on the minds of my teachers and parents, too. The reason I am a part of this book is that I applied the four success principles that I wrote about in this book.

Even though it took a lot of courage for me to drop out of school and go against what society expected of me, I saw the prospect of becoming an author as a chance for me to turn my academic challenges into an opportunity. Most people think that to become published you have to be a good writer. After meeting with our writing coach and mentor, David Strauss, I realized that if I can leverage my weaknesses with his strengths, it would be a shoe-in for my ideas to be published. I knew I had an important message to share. I just needed help to get my ideas out of my mind and onto paper.

In school, if someone helps you with your exams it is considered cheating. In the world of entrepreneurs, your success comes from finding people who are smarter than you and having them help you to win. Instead of stressing out about not being a great writer, I decided to double down on what I am good at and leverage my weaknesses. My strength is my ability to think quickly and consume new ideas efficiently. I am also good at expressing my ideas verbally. Working with someone who could fill in the gap of getting my ideas into writing allowed me to overcome my barricade so that my story and voice could be heard.

Whether or not someone finishes school, they are still a product of the school system. One of the unforeseen consequences of the educational system is that a kid's self-esteem can be negatively affected by the grading system. If someone like me does not learn the way the system teaches, it is easy to take bad grades personally and think that there is something wrong with them. If schools were better at identifying each kid's native genius and the way they like to learn and adapted to different ways of teaching, kids would be empowered to grow up and be more creative and productive.

Something that caught me by surprise after leaving school is when I learned that there are a lot of famous people who did not graduate high school.

Charlie Sheen never graduated from high school. He was only a few weeks from graduation when he dropped out because of bad grades and attendance.

Jim Carrey never graduated high school. He came from poverty and was forced to drop out of school so he could help take care of his sick mom. He began performing at comedy clubs and eventually was cast in a television series at age 18. He is now considered one of the funniest people in the world.

John Travolta left high school to study acting, dancing, and singing. His first big break, which opened the door for his now famous career, happened when he was 21 when he was cast for the television show, "Welcome Back, Kotter."

Other actors, actresses, and entertainers who never finished high school include Al Pacino, Marilyn Monroe, Hilary Swank, Aretha Franklin, and Eminem, who never made it past ninth grade.

If you did not finish school, you might think that you are in good company. What sets them apart is that when the going got tough, they got focused. They turned their failures and setbacks into drive, ambition, and motivation.

I am not saying that kids should not finish school. They definitely should when all the conditions are right for them. The point is that everyone has a hidden talent, something that they are born with which makes them unique. If we learn how to identify and tap into a person's strengths when they are young, think about how different our world would become. Kids would grow up and walk around with a greater sense of purpose and personal pride, instead of so many feeling lost and without focus. Kids do not get involved in drugs or other self-destructive behaviors because they want to, but because they do not have a solid identity or strong self-image, so they do what they can to gain attention, be liked by others, and to fit in.

Being a part of this book was important to me for a few reasons. Even though I had a lot of growing up to do and had to burn through some big challenges to make this happen, one of my key motivations is that I wanted to get in the face of other kids in our generation (Generation Y) and tell them that we do not have to accept things as they are. We can be the generation that begins to make a difference in the world. We are holding the entire universe in the palms of our hands with our smartphones. We can learn anything we want to learn from any location that has an internet connection. Let's learn how to make a difference.

I want to challenge our generation, and anyone else that relates to this book, to get off your ass and do something to improve our world. There is no excuse for the problems of the world to persist given the technology we have.

As a generation, and pretty much everyone else, we have lots of problems to work through. Our environment is a wreck. Too many kids are going to bed hungry. Student loan debt is making intelligent minds a slave to banks, and everyone is being told that they need to be equal and the same instead of learning how to unleash their uniqueness and inner power. Instead of growing up to be strong and confident, a lot of kids are being raised to feel emotionally weak and entitled. Everyone wants a trophy, but not everyone wants to do what it takes to win. Politicians and the news are lying to the public and then lying about their lies. This mockery of humanity cannot go on forever; it is not sustainable.

We cannot change everything, but we can change the way we think. We can start to apply principles of success and make headway toward improving our world. If we do not do something now, the problems of our parents are going to be passed down to us, and will only get worse.

We have a big journey ahead of us, but we are the smartest generation ever. We have immediate access to more tools and resources to make a difference than any other time in history. We do not see the world the same way as previous generations. We have grown up in a world that is changing rapidly. We think on our feet. We get information instantly. We do not have to wait to communicate or to learn. Everything is in the palm of our hands.

We are the reason why things can get better for everyone, but it is not going to happen if we waste this golden opportunity by using social media and the internet for instant gratification and mindless activities.

What is it going to take for our generation and everyone else who cares about the direction of humanity to wake up and pay attention to how we are screwing ourselves? Politicians are not our problem. Government is not our problem. Our challenge is to learn how to take responsibility for ourselves and each other, to learn how to develop critical thinking, and to become leaders, not followers.

The world that our parents grew up in does not exist anymore. We cannot apply old, unsuccessful thinking to the same problems that have yet to be solved. We are the next leaders of the world. We are setting new trends. Not too long ago a lot of people believed social media was a waste of time, but now people realize it is a way to gather around ideas and make things happen.

Our generation understands social media better than anyone else. We have to start making the problems of the world our own. We cannot wait for the older generation to solve them. If they could, they would have already. Let's create solutions never imagined before. But it starts with you. Before you can improve the world, you must first work on yourself, your family, and your community. Change always starts locally, and from there it expands out to the whole world.

If we come together and cultivate a family environment that is not focused on race, sex, or any other labeled group, and start to treat each other as humans rather than categories of humans, that is when we will begin to create momentum toward improving our world.

It is time to set aside our differences and focus on what we are good at. How can each of us do our part to create solutions to local and global challenges? There is enough talent, uniqueness and diversity for us to fix what is not working and build upon what is working. Stop focusing on regulations and start focusing on innovations. If we turn our problems into opportunities, we may finally have peace!

Ask yourself these four questions, and you will figure where you fit into the puzzle.

- What am I good at?
- What difference do I want to make in the world?
- Why do I want to make a difference?
- How can I make a difference doing what I am good at?

Think!

Acknowledgements

It is still surreal to me that a high school dropout could become a published author in his early 20s. The only reason this happened is that I did not let my past hold me back. Instead, it motivated me to find out who I am and what I am truly capable of, and it catapulted me on a quest to find people who could teach me what I wanted to learn.

I wish I could take credit for the success of being a part of this book. Ultimately, the reason it happened is because of four people in my life who have shaped and inspired me—my mom and dad; my mentor, Michelle Barnes; and our writing coach and mentor, David Strauss.

MOM—CYNTHIA DARLENE WRIGHT

How can anyone even begin to thank their mother when there is so much to be grateful for? Mom, you have been my biggest fan. You have supported me through every endeavor in my life. You defended me countless times, even when sometimes I did not deserve it. You are the one who taught me what it means to have resilience, and you inspired me to be more compassionate and caring in my life. You never once wavered in your faith in the Lord, and your strong foundation in spiritual beliefs is why I have a relationship with our Lord and Savior today. You have been willing to sacrifice everything that you have to see your children just smile and be happy. For all of that and more, I will never be able to repay you.

With my deepest sincerity, you are the sweetest and most caring person I have ever met. Most everything I am today is because of you. You have made this world such a better place because of who you are. You are my source of strength as well as my source of peace when I need it. Thank you for everything you have ever done. This goes without saying: I love you!

DAD—JOHN EDWARD WRIGHT

Dad, first of all, thank you for giving me life. All jokes aside, I appreciate your wisdom and guidance. Never in my life have I ever met somebody who thinks as big as you do. I have always been amazed at your understanding of how the world truly works and that you have never been afraid to talk to your children as the adults you want them to become. Thank you for all the times you spent countless hours helping me out by practicing sports with me. You have been an excellent role model of what it means to be a family man, and through your example, you have shown me what it means to be a genuine father. You have always done whatever it takes to support our family. It has not always been easy, but you have always made it happen. I love you, and I want you to know that I would not be growing into the young man I am today without you as my father.

MICHELLE BARNES—MENTOR

Thanks for being fun! You taught me how to bring energy and humor to a room full of people and how to draw their attention and keep them on the edge of their seats. Most importantly, you opened up my mind to the importance of networking and creating authentic connections. You taught me not to burn bridges because you never know where you are going to be in five years, and it is better to leave a positive impression than a negative memory. You have changed the lives of thousands of people. I am thankful that I was one of them.

DAVID STRAUSS—*THINK GEN WHY* COACH AND MENTOR

David saw something in all of us that we did not see in ourselves. He saw hope for a future generation, he believed in us and our potential, and he wanted to give that hope and potential a voice. Thank you for your patience and understanding to help make this book a reality.

When I first met David, I had never met someone with his level of openness about their personal story. He was an open book about what had happened to him in his life. He would tell you stuff that most people would never imagine letting other people know. He shared the harsh lessons he had learned from his near-death experience, along with some tough challenges he faced while growing up. David spoke about them with zero hesitation, which made me realize that for him to be able to talk so freely, it meant he was no longer affected by his past. Most people can say they have gotten over stuff or moved on, but until meeting David, I had never met someone who had.

ACKNOWLEDGEMENTS

David's openness is a big reason why we were able to write this book. He taught us that instead of being a victim of your past, you have to own your personal story with pride, and when you overcome your past pains, the lessons learned become your credentials to help other people. That realization proved to me that if you want to put stuff behind you, you first have to face your problems head-on and turn your challenges into opportunities.

On behalf of all the other authors of this book, I would like to thank David for his patience and understanding throughout the whole process, from beginning to being published. Without you, we would not have been able to persevere through this journey of becoming authors.

What I am most blessed by is the fact that God put you in my life at such a young age. I look forward to a very long friendship!

Finally, there are my boys, Ryan, Kyler, Matthew, and Ethan, and my brother Jesse, who are my friends and family for life and co-authors of this book. We are going to rock this world.

#ThinkGenWhy

Enjoyed this book?
Share the love...
Tweet, post, Insta...
#ThinkGenWhy
Facebook.com/ThinkGenWhy

Review on Amazon. Go to:
www.ThinkGenWhyBook.com

Afterword

Think Gen Why is more than a book. It is the beginning of a movement inspired by the idea that everyone has unlimited potential that can be unlocked by unraveling limiting beliefs and replacing them with thoughts and ideas that supercharge individuality, and ignite confidence, purpose, and passion.

As co-authors of this book, we challenge our readers to take a close look in the mirror and ask yourselves if you are living up to your potential, or hiding behind past hurts and pains disguised as self-doubt?

Ask yourself these questions. If you truly believed in yourself and had all the confidence that you needed to create your ideal life, what would you do with your time on this planet? What would you want to create? What difference would you want to make in the world? What impression would you want to make upon others? What wrongs would you want to make right? What legacy would you want to leave behind?

If you do not have the confidence to shape your own reality, what will it take for you to gain that self-belief? What will it take for you to grab life by the balls and say yes to what you *do* want and no to what you *do not* want? What will it take for you to defy the odds, set a new standard for yourself, and step up to your true power?

Life is not going to wait for you to figure things out. The clock is always ticking. Time does not stand still as you contemplate your reality. Decide what you want. Decide what makes you feel loved, fulfilled, and happy, and pursue your life with uninhibited belief.

It is time for all of us to stop playing small.

- Stop pretending that it is okay to go through life half-awake with a mediocre attitude.
- Stop living in the shadows of giants and begin to love yourself and discover your own greatness.
- Stop waiting for permission to do something different. You do not need permission. You only need courage.
- Stop waiting for life to change so that you do not have to. Become flexible in your beliefs and adjust your mindset.
- Stop believing that life is happening to you. You are a part of life. It is happening through you and as you.
- Stop living the illusion that you are powerless over your circumstances. Your power is hidden in your ability to let go of the past, think clearly, and take action.
- Stop holding onto the skeletons in your closet. Let go of limiting beliefs and transform your weaknesses into strengths.
- Stop blaming society, your parents, or anything that has happened to you for your problems or insecurities. You decide the meaning of your life experiences. You decide the ending to the story of your life.
- Stop looking outside of yourself for answers. Everything that you are looking for can be found within your own heart and mind. You are the answer.

Think Gen Why is a wake-up call. It is time to realize that your past does not determine your future. The current circumstances of your life are nothing more than the effects of your old way of thinking, and old choices and habits. You are not stuck unless you think you are. Your past is not a life sentence. Your prior experiences are lessons in the classroom of life. The people you met and interacted with are the teachers, and you get to decide the lessons that you want to extract from those experiences.

If you are inspired by the content of this book, then keep it close to you and use it as a tool to help you on your journey. You can change your life. You can chart a new course and set a new destination for the remainder of your life. Choose the lessons that you identify with most strongly and integrate them into your life. Find *Think Gen Why* on social media, and reach out to the authors who have had the greatest impact on your thinking. Tell them stories about how your life has changed.

At the end of the day, the meaning of your life is the meaning you have chosen. Choose wisely. Become a thinker. Think for yourself. Learn how to think accurately and strategically. Inspire your generation and generations to come. Find your *why*. Find out what motivates and inspires you, and be your ideal self.

Join The

THINK GEN WHY

MOVEMENT

Learn How to Improve Your Thinking.

Like & Follow Us:

Facebook.Com/Thinkgenwhy
YouTube.Com/Thinkgenwhy
Instagram/@Thinkgenwhy

Book Us To Speak At Your Event:

Www.ThinkGenWhy.Com/Connect

A Call to Action

Think Gen Why is a personal challenge to change your life by changing your thinking. It is also a challenge to improve our world.

When you look at the human condition, it is easy to become discouraged about the future. The amount of personal suffering on this planet is inexcusable. Far too many people are deprived of love, self-worth, and the basic necessities of life. Given the amount of food and natural resources on this planet, there is no reason for anyone to live a life of deprivation. There is no reason for children to be starving. There is no reason for people to live in filth and disease, and there is no excuse for the epic volumes of reckless pollution. There is no reason, other than we have deflected responsibility and made it someone else's problem to solve. We have mentally and emotionally distanced ourselves from the disaster we have created, and desensitized ourselves to the repercussions of our collective neglect.

While most of the world is trying to figure out what happened and how we got to a point in time where there is so much in-fighting amongst humanity, we believe the solution to all problems is awareness.

It is time for things to change. It is time for us to acknowledge that the heart and mind of humanity is ready for a system upgrade. We are ready for a new approach to life, a new vision in which we are awakened to our responsibility for ourselves and each other.

Instead of looking at the world with shock, tears, and disgust, let's begin to re-educate people, especially our youth, to believe in themselves. Let's create a movement of inspiration and enthusiasm that brings an end to the victim mindset that has cast a shadow over humanity, and replace it with a new way of thinking that leads to a stronger sense of self-worth, purpose, and self-love. Let's inspire people to take positive, meaningful actions to restore the planet and humanity to its natural place of peace, love, and harmony.

With so many people looking to point blame, let's look in the mirror and point to ourselves because through our choices, individually and collectively, we are responsible for the conditions of our world. Let's replace blame with a new way of thinking that encourages personal responsibility and solution-oriented thinking.

We are reaching an upsurge in poverty, disease, and planetary destruction that may be irreversible, but it does not have to be that way. The awareness that we need to develop to solve these problems is to remember that we are all energetically connected. At our core, we are all a part of humanity, not apart from it. It is our thinking that is causing the problems. We need to wake up and start thinking and acting like a global community instead of pockets of differences pursuing our own self-interests. All of the pushing-against each-other, all of the focus on our differences, perpetuates fear and scarcity and advances our self destruction.

The time has come for us to wake up. We are responsible for our own choices, and for the effect that our choices have on each other and on our planet. We cannot pollute the oceans and not have it affect our food and water supply. We cannot bomb one part of the earth and not have it affect the entire planet. What we do to others, we do to ourselves.

Just as sunlight awakens a flower at the dawn of a new day, awareness is the solution that will awaken humanity.

- The awareness begins by recognizing that we are more alike than we are different. We are a diverse pool of uniquely different humans. Outwardly, we are different. Inwardly, we are the same.
- It begins with simple coffee talk amongst friends and family where we discuss new ideas about how to better our world and how to implement those ideas locally.
- It begins by creating a sense of community and doing things together to improve our neighborhoods, parks, and schools.
- It begins by being friendly to the people with whom we interact on a daily basis and treating them with kindness.
- It begins when we look at what we have in common rather than our differences.
- It begins when we discard our self-defeating story and create a new vision for who we are.
- It begins with having the courage to let go of obsolete thinking and developing a fresh vision for your life.

Our solutions begin with each of us, individually. As you connect with your personal power, the positive effects will become contagious and begin to infect others with a desire to grow and improve.

The call to action is very simple.

GET OFF YOUR ASS AND DO SOMETHING DIFFERENT!

About the Coach

David Strauss is the producer and publisher of *Think Gen Why*, and the coach that helped these six young men share their ideas.

In 2016 David attended several entrepreneur seminars in Denver and Las Vegas. At each of these seminars, he noticed a group of sharply dressed young men who were enthusiastic about learning. He couldn't help but be curious what these guys were about. After taking the initiative to get to know them, David realized that these young men had an above-average mindset and had something meaningful to contribute to society.

In a conversation with Jesse Wright, one of the authors, David suggested that they join forces and write a book together. Within a few weeks, that suggestion quickly became a reality.

David saw tremendous value in helping these young men become authors because he recognized the importance of their personal story. David knows, from his own experience, that when you tell your life story to others, with all its beauty and ugly challenges, you give permission to others to have the courage to tell their story. If your story is one of personal transformation and triumph, then your courage enables others to transform, too.

Even though David is an internationally recognized author, speaker, thought leader, and results coach, you would not know that when you first meet him. David has been humbled by unforeseen challenges in his life, and he has not forgotten where he came from.

At the early age of 15, David lost his mother to a brain tumor. His family quickly fell apart which left him feeling alone and isolated. With no one there to help him sort through his confusion, he ran away from home and began to take responsibility for his own life. Unlike most runaways, David put himself through high school and college and continuously challenged himself to learn and grow by seeking out mentors to help him expand his awareness.

Later in David's life, he faced the possibility of his death after being hit on the head by a falling rock. Through his journey of healing from his rock collision, David discovered his true sense of purpose. He has connected with a singular vision of wanting to have a lasting and meaningful impact on people's lives by challenging them to take 100% responsibility for their life experiences and for their happiness.

Recognizing the value of learning from experience, David's vision of wanting to inspire others first started becoming a reality through the release of his first book, *Footsteps After the Fall,* and through the development of the Giggle Yoga Project. He extended his reach in his second book, *Dancing with Vampires,* which teaches people how to take responsibility for their lives and rid themselves of negative influences.

Having survived the rock experience, along with years of travel and life adventures and learning from many of his mistakes, David developed a treasure chest of insightful tools for speaking, coaching, and mentoring. He believes that everyone has a book in them—a personal story which, if properly tuned like a fine instrument, can inspire others and have a positive impact on the human spirit. This belief is what inspired him to want to help the authors of this book share their story.

Behind David's voice and message is a sense of deep insight, wisdom, and intuition from a very diverse life. He understands that we are all responsible for the meaning we give to our life experiences. Most importantly, we can change the effects of our past by changing our story—by changing the meaning we give to our life events. When we make this change, the entire trajectory of our life changes.

As an outgrowth of his desire to help others improve their lives, David is continually looking for ways to create strategic relationships with other people, businesses, and thought leaders who are dedicated to improving the overall direction and welfare of humanity. As such, David recently spoke at the Global Entrepreneurship Initiative at the United Nations Headquarters in New York City where he talked about the importance of having a mentor. David has also been seen on ABC, NBC, CBS, and FOX affiliate TV networks where he was interviewed by Bob Guiney, Oprah's man on the street and a star on the TV show, "The Bachelor."

All of David's work can be whittled down to the core messages of personal responsibility, forgiveness, and gratitude.

| DavidStrauss.com

THANK YOU TO OUR SPONSORS

And to those who have supported the creation of this book.

Christine Chacon
Danielle Dampier
Hunter Noell
Jonathan Castner, Photographer
Lara Ortiz
Lindsey Jaffe
Lynn Graff
Martha Miller
Morgan Horsley
Pro Painters, LLC
Sam, Inc.
Sarah Frank
Sharon Pera
The Giggle Yoga Project
The Shreves
Tony Grebmeier
Wally Weckbaugh – WEB Commercial Group, Denver, CO
Western Safety Supply

Suggested Reading

Now that you have finished reading our book, if you are ready to enter the journey of personal growth, we suggest that you fall in love with reading.

Here are a few of the books that we highly recommend.

- *Dancing with Vampires* – By David Lloyd Strauss
- *Greatest Salesman in the World* – By Og Mandino
- *How to Win Friends and Influence People* – By Dale Carnegie
- *Law of Success* – By Napoleon Hill
- *Richest Man in Babylon* – By George S. Clason
- *The Power of Habit* – By Charles Duhigg
- *The Power of Now* – By Eckhart Tolle
- *Think and Grow Rich* – By Napoleon Hill
- *What to Say When You Talk to Yourself* – By Shad Helmstetter

www.ingramcontent.com/pod-product-compliance
Lightning Source LLC
Chambersburg PA
CBHW070558300426
44113CB00010B/1299